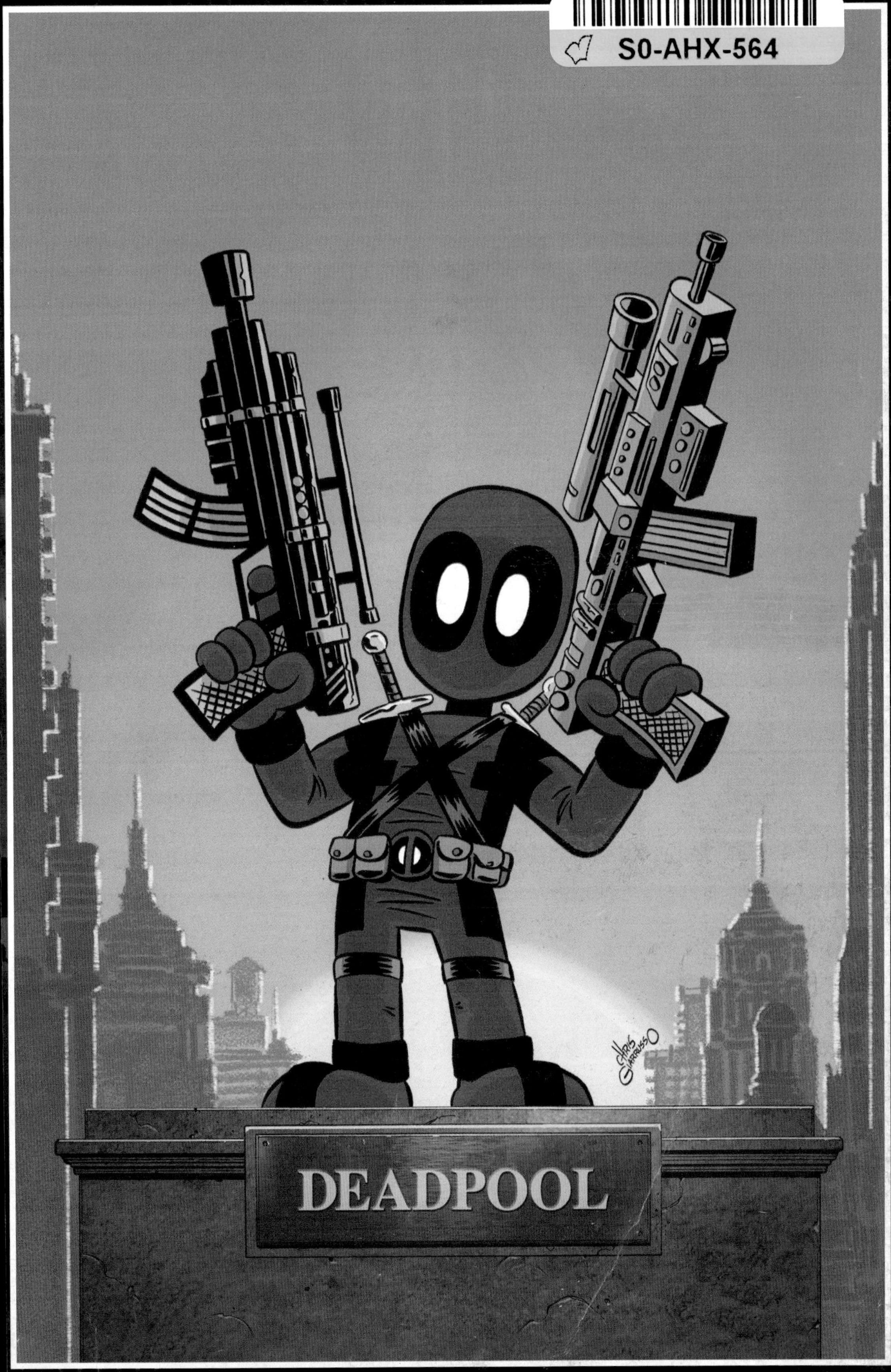
DEADPOOL
CHRIS GIARRUSSO

DEADPOOL #23 HEROIC AGE VARIANT
by Chris Giarrusso

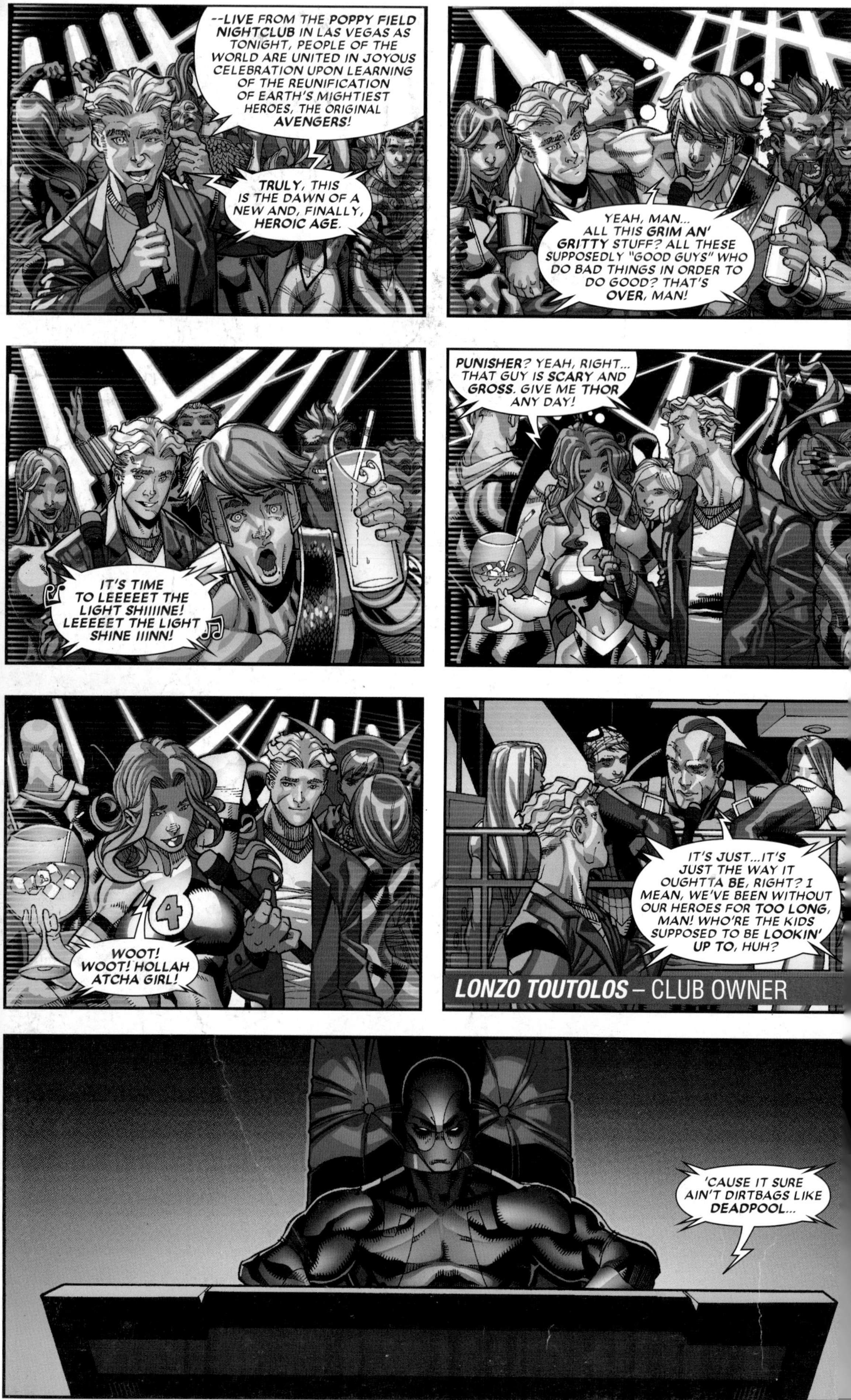
--LIVE FROM THE POPPY FIELD NIGHTCLUB IN LAS VEGAS AS TONIGHT, PEOPLE OF THE WORLD ARE UNITED IN JOYOUS CELEBRATION UPON LEARNING OF THE REUNIFICATION OF EARTH'S MIGHTIEST HEROES, THE ORIGINAL AVENGERS!
TRULY, THIS IS THE DAWN OF A NEW AND, FINALLY, HEROIC AGE.
YEAH, MAN... ALL THIS GRIM AN' GRITTY STUFF? ALL THESE SUPPOSEDLY "GOOD GUYS" WHO DO BAD THINGS IN ORDER TO DO GOOD? THAT'S OVER, MAN!
IT'S TIME TO LEEEEET THE LIGHT SHIIIINE! LEEEEET THE LIGHT SHINE IIINN!
PUNISHER? YEAH, RIGHT... THAT GUY IS SCARY AND GROSS. GIVE ME THOR ANY DAY!
WOOT! WOOT! HOLLAH ATCHA GIRL!
IT'S JUST...IT'S JUST THE WAY IT OUGHTTA BE, RIGHT? I MEAN, WE'VE BEEN WITHOUT OUR HEROES FOR TOO LONG, MAN! WHO'RE THE KIDS SUPPOSED TO BE LOOKIN' UP TO, HUH?
LONZO TOUTOLOS – CLUB OWNER
'CAUSE IT SURE AIN'T DIRTBAGS LIKE DEADPOOL...

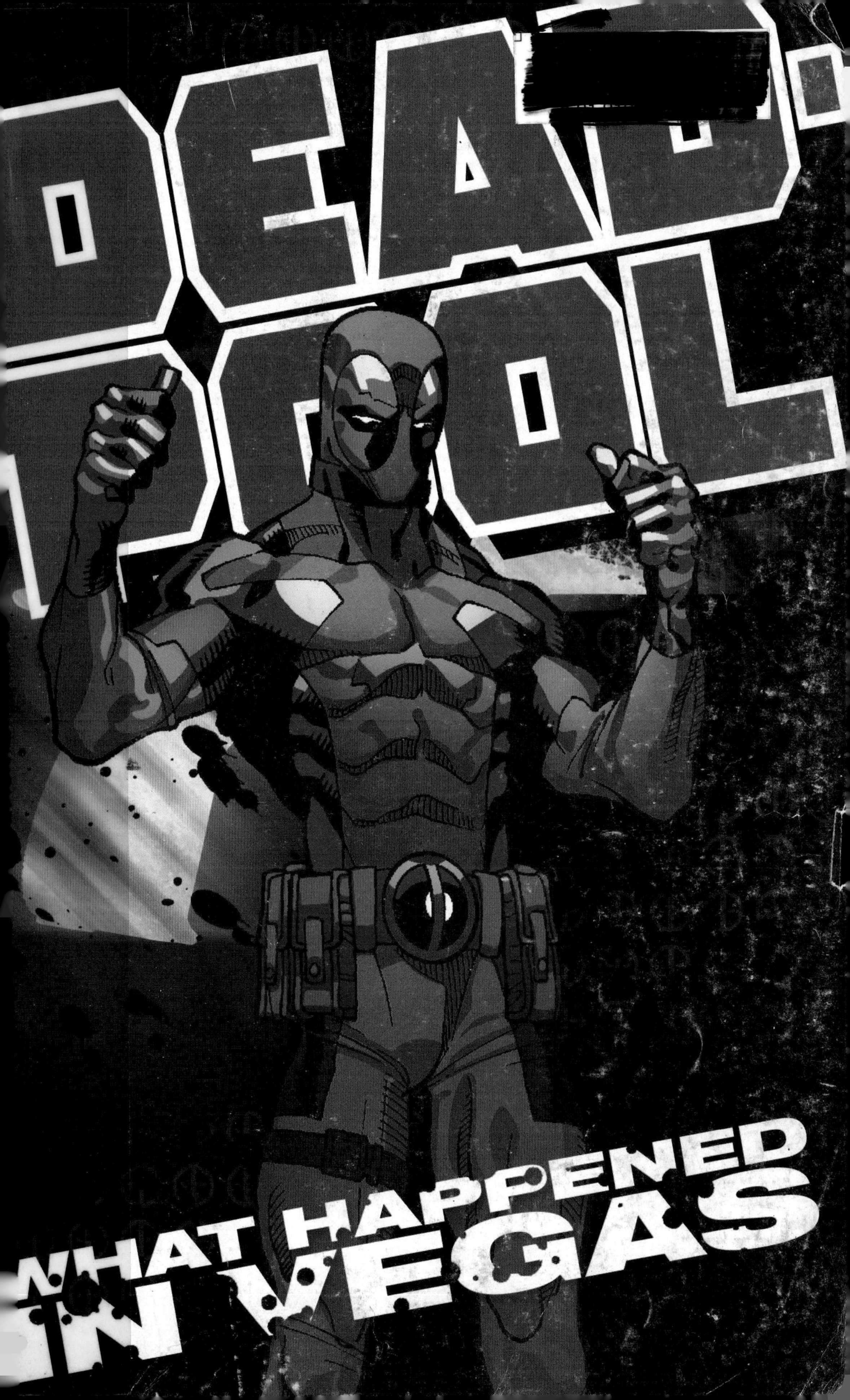
DEA[redacted]
POOL
WHAT HAPPENED
IN VEGAS

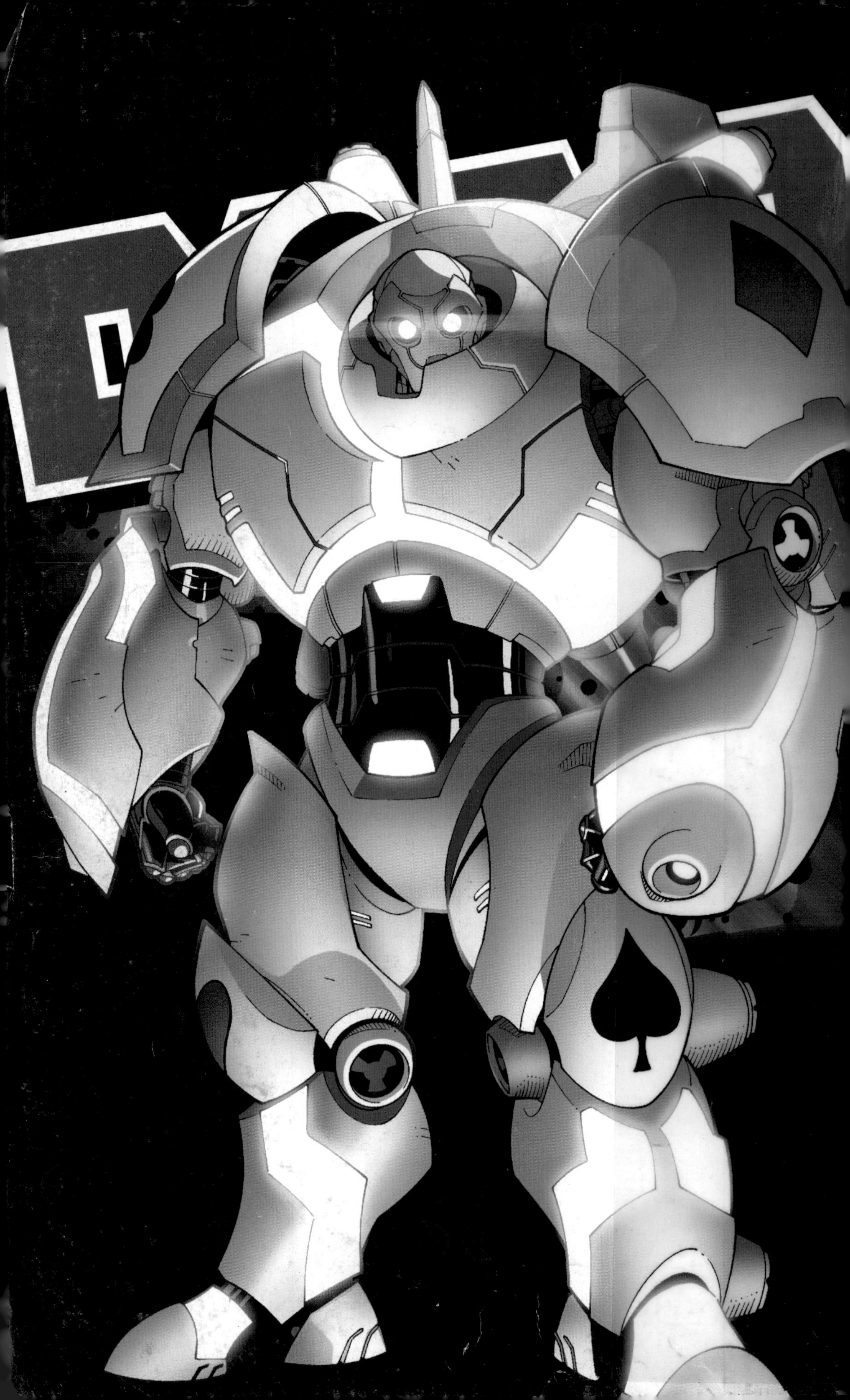

POOL
WHAT HAPPENED IN VEGAS

WRITER: **DANIEL WAY** • PENCILS: **CARLO BARBERI**
INKS: **JUAN VLASCO** • COLORS: **MARTE GRACIA**
LETTERS: **VIRTUAL CALLIGRAPHY'S JOE SABINO**
COVER ARTISTS: **JASON PEARSON & DAVE JOHNSON**

"WADE UNTIL DARK"
WRITER: **DUANE SWIERCZYNSKI** • ART: **PHILIP BOND**
COLORS: **LEE LOUGHRIDGE**
LETTERS: **VIRTUAL CALLIGRAPHY'S JOE SABINO**

ASSISTANT EDITOR: **JODY LEHEUP**
EDITOR: **AXEL ALONSO**

COLLECTION EDITOR: **CORY LEVINE**
EDITORIAL ASSISTANTS: **JAMES EMMETT & JOE HOCHSTEIN**
ASSISTANT EDITORS: **ALEX STARBUCK & NELSON RIBEIRO**
EDITORS, SPECIAL PROJECTS: **JENNIFER GRÜNWALD & MARK D. BEAZLEY**
SENIOR EDITOR, SPECIAL PROJECTS: **JEFF YOUNGQUIST**
SENIOR VICE PRESIDENT OF SALES: **DAVID GABRIEL**
BOOK DESIGN: **RODOLFO MURAGUCHI**

EDITOR IN CHIEF: **JOE QUESADA**
PUBLISHER: **DAN BUCKLEY**
EXECUTIVE PRODUCER: **ALAN FINE**

DEADPOOL VOL. 5: WHAT HAPPENED IN VEGAS. Contains material originally published in magazine form as DEADPOOL #23-26. First printing 2010. Hardcover ISBN# 978-0-7851-4532-5. Softcover ISBN# 978-0-7851-4533-2. Published by MARVEL WORLDWIDE, INC., a subsidiary of MARVEL ENTERTAINMENT, LLC. OFFICE OF PUBLICATION: 417 5th Avenue, New York, NY 10016. Copyright © 2010 and 2011 Marvel Characters, Inc. All rights reserved. Hardcover: $19.99 per copy in the U.S. and $22.50 in Canada (GST #R127032852). Softcover: $15.99 per copy in the U.S. and $17.99 in Canada (GST #R127032852). Canadian Agreement #40668537. All characters featured in this issue and the distinctive names and likenesses thereof, and all related indicia are trademarks of Marvel Characters, Inc. No similarity between any of the names, characters, persons, and/or institutions in this magazine with those of any living or dead person or institution is intended, and any such similarity which may exist is purely coincidental. **Printed in the U.S.A.** ALAN FINE, EVP - Office of the President, Marvel Worldwide, Inc. and EVP & CMO Marvel Characters B.V.; DAN BUCKLEY, Chief Executive Officer and Publisher - Print, Animation & Digital Media; JIM SOKOLOWSKI, Chief Operating Officer; DAVID GABRIEL, SVP of Publishing Sales & Circulation; DAVID BOGART, SVP of Business Affairs & Talent Management; MICHAEL PASCIULLO, VP Merchandising & Communications; JIM O'KEEFE, VP of Operations & Logistics; DAN CARR, Executive Director of Publishing Technology; JUSTIN F. GABRIE, Director of Publishing & Editorial Operations; SUSAN CRESPI, Editorial Operations Manager; ALEX MORALES, Publishing Operations Manager; STAN LEE, Chairman Emeritus. For information regarding advertising in Marvel Comics or on Marvel.com, please contact Ron Stern, VP of Business Development, at rstern@marvel.com. For Marvel subscription inquiries, please call 800-217-9158. **Manufactured between** 8/30/10 and 9/29/10 (hardcover), and 8/30/10 and 2/23/11 (softcover), by R.R. DONNELLEY, INC., SALEM, VA, USA.

10 9 8 7 6 5 4 3 2 1

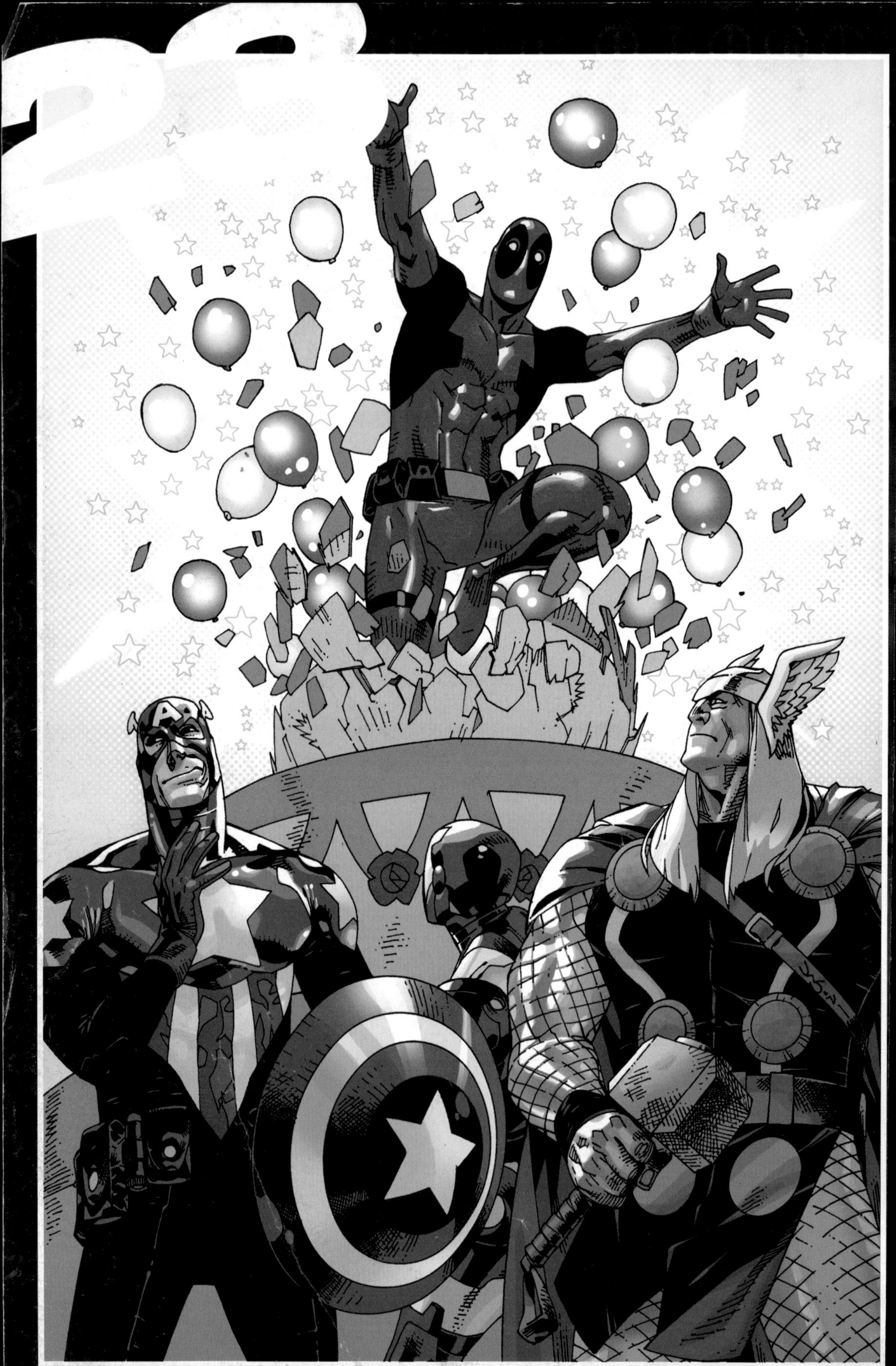

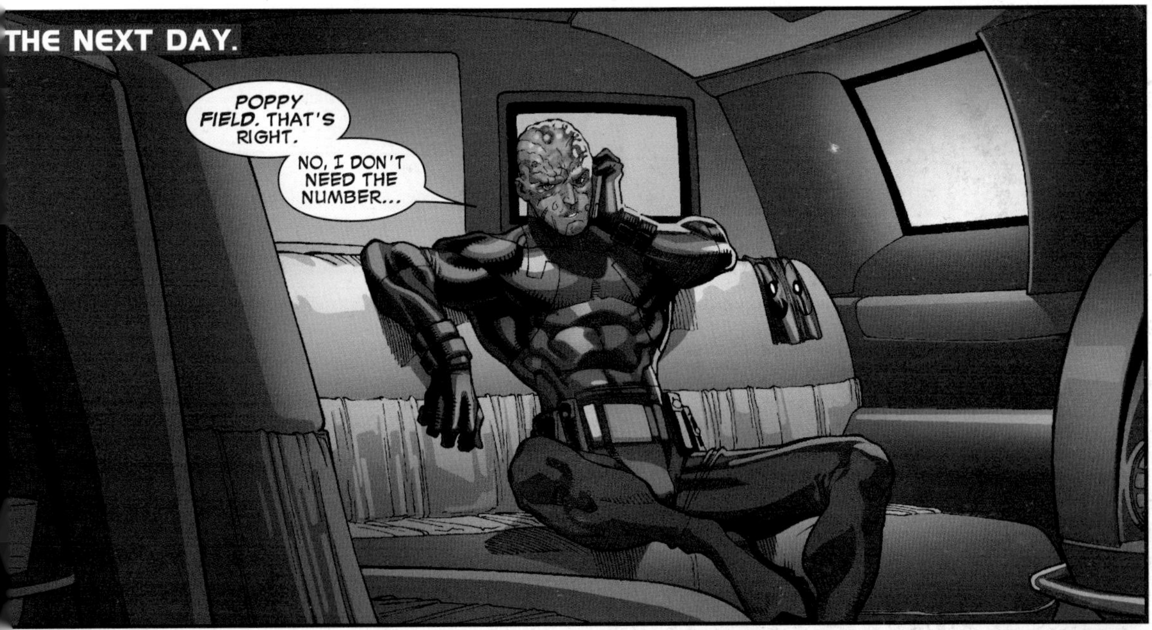
THE NEXT DAY.
POPPY FIELD. THAT'S RIGHT.
NO, I DON'T NEED THE NUMBER...

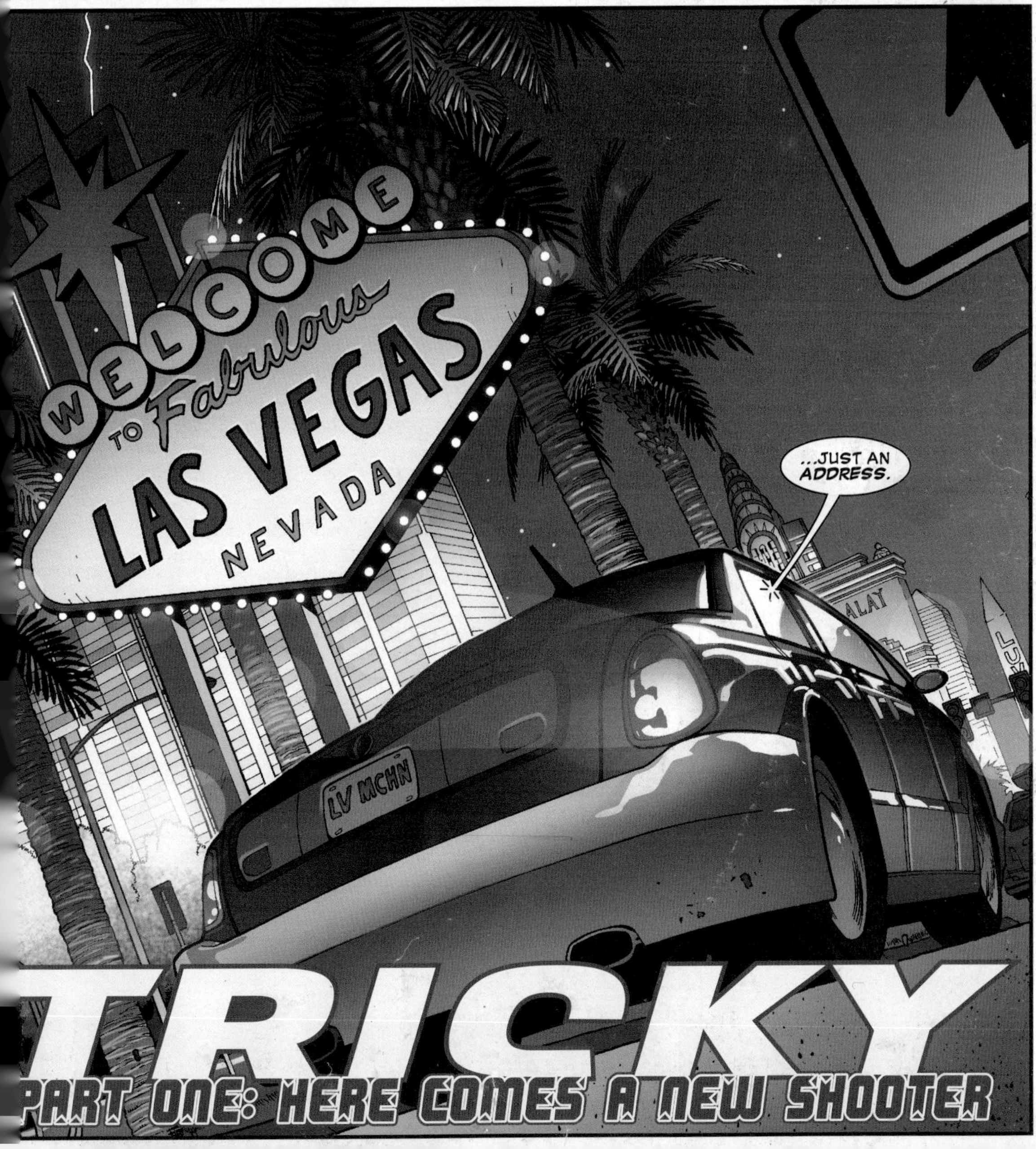
WELCOME TO Fabulous LAS VEGAS NEVADA
...JUST AN ADDRESS.
LV MCHN
TRICKY
PART ONE: HERE COMES A NEW SHOOTER

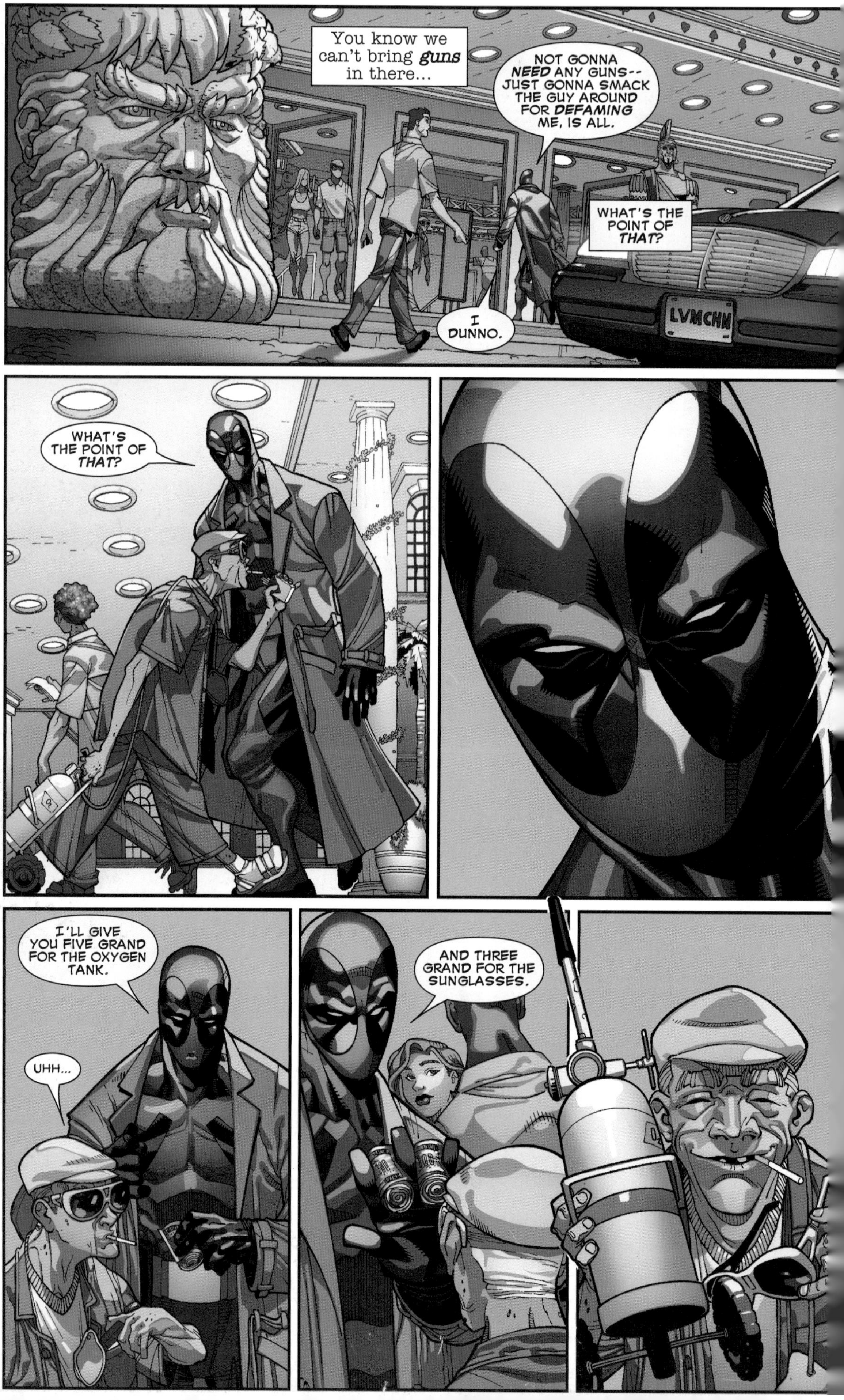

You know we can't bring *guns* in there...
NOT GONNA *NEED* ANY GUNS-- JUST GONNA SMACK THE GUY AROUND FOR *DEFAMING* ME, IS ALL.
WHAT'S THE POINT OF *THAT*?
I DUNNO.
LVMCHN
WHAT'S THE POINT OF *THAT*?
I'LL GIVE YOU FIVE GRAND FOR THE OXYGEN TANK.
UHH...
AND THREE GRAND FOR THE SUNGLASSES.

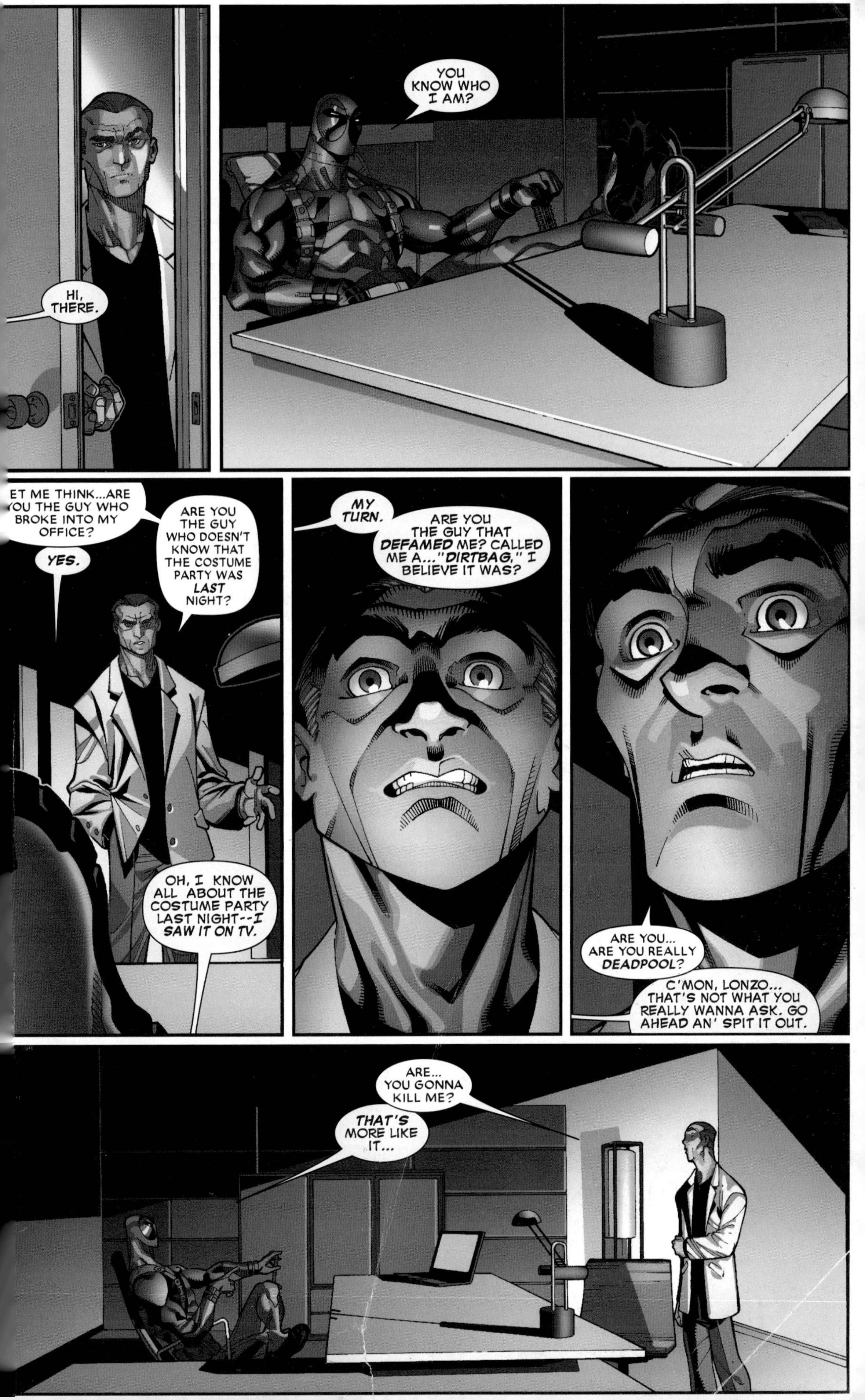

HI, THERE.
YOU KNOW WHO I AM?
ET ME THINK...ARE YOU THE GUY WHO BROKE INTO MY OFFICE?
YES.
ARE YOU THE GUY WHO DOESN'T KNOW THAT THE COSTUME PARTY WAS LAST NIGHT?
OH, I KNOW ALL ABOUT THE COSTUME PARTY LAST NIGHT--I SAW IT ON TV.
MY TURN.
ARE YOU THE GUY THAT DEFAMED ME? CALLED ME A..."DIRTBAG," I BELIEVE IT WAS?
ARE YOU... ARE YOU REALLY DEADPOOL?
C'MON, LONZO... THAT'S NOT WHAT YOU REALLY WANNA ASK. GO AHEAD AN' SPIT IT OUT.
ARE... YOU GONNA KILL ME?
THAT'S MORE LIKE IT...

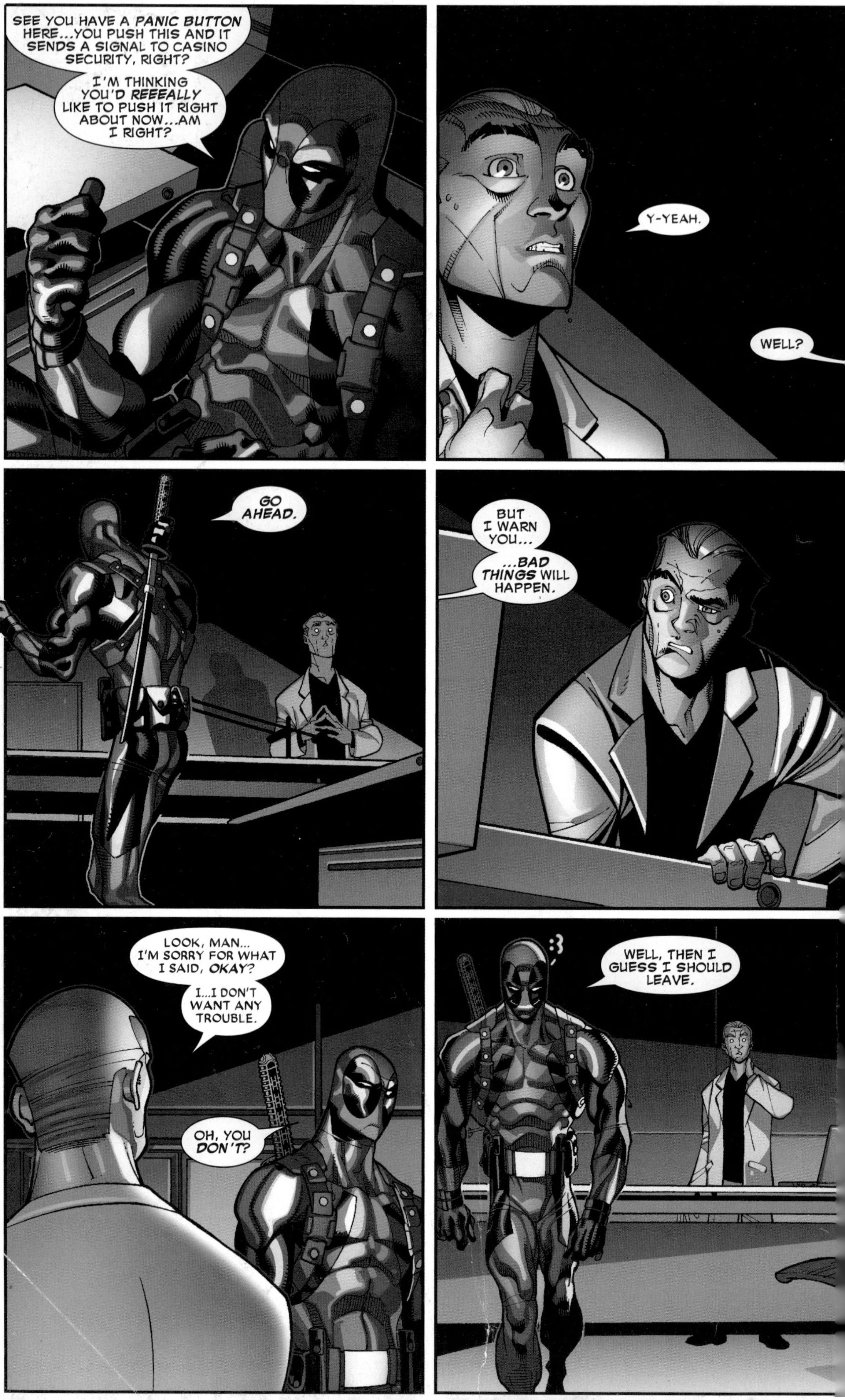
SEE YOU HAVE A PANIC BUTTON HERE...YOU PUSH THIS AND IT SENDS A SIGNAL TO CASINO SECURITY, RIGHT?
I'M THINKING YOU'D REEEALLY LIKE TO PUSH IT RIGHT ABOUT NOW...AM I RIGHT?
Y-YEAH.
WELL?
GO AHEAD.
BUT I WARN YOU...
...BAD THINGS WILL HAPPEN.
LOOK, MAN... I'M SORRY FOR WHAT I SAID, OKAY?
I...I DON'T WANT ANY TROUBLE.
OH, YOU DON'T?
WELL, THEN I GUESS I SHOULD LEAVE.

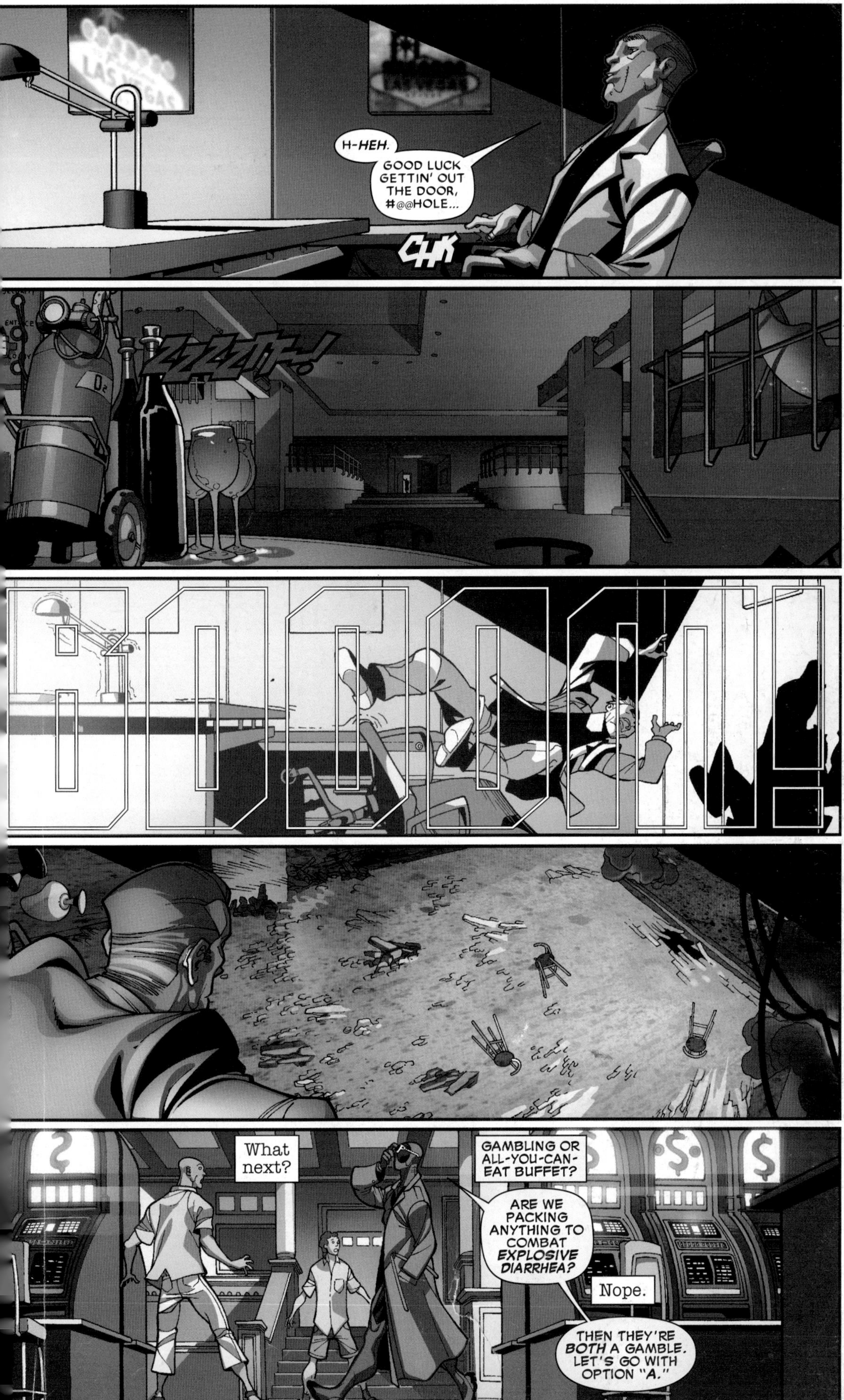
H-HEH.
GOOD LUCK GETTIN' OUT THE DOOR, #@@HOLE...
CHK
ZZZZWOP-!
BOOOOM!
What next?
GAMBLING OR ALL-YOU-CAN-EAT BUFFET?
ARE WE PACKING ANYTHING TO COMBAT EXPLOSIVE DIARRHEA?
Nope.
THEN THEY'RE BOTH A GAMBLE. LET'S GO WITH OPTION "A."

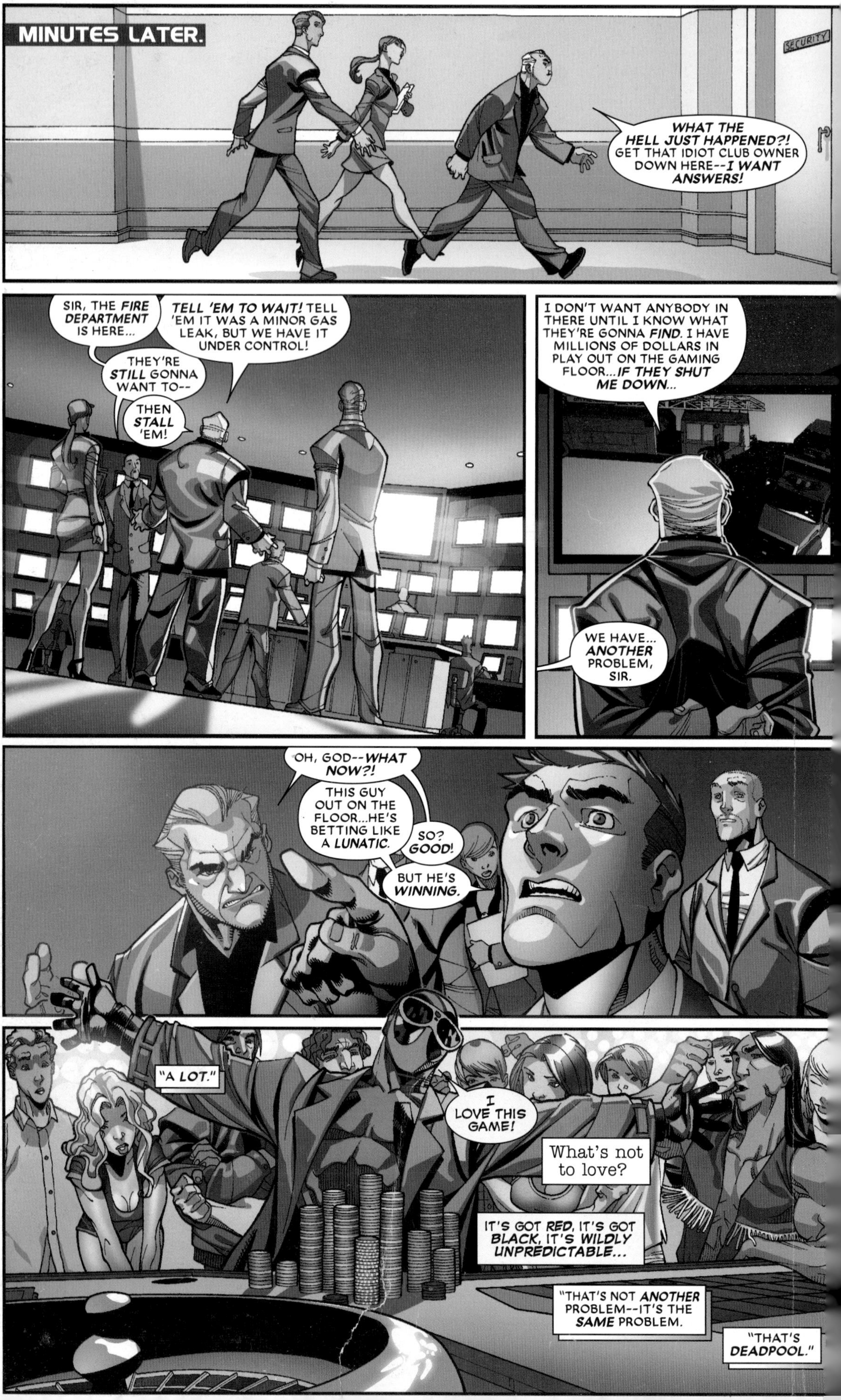
MINUTES LATER.
SECURITY
WHAT THE HELL JUST HAPPENED?! GET THAT IDIOT CLUB OWNER DOWN HERE--I WANT ANSWERS!
SIR, THE FIRE DEPARTMENT IS HERE...
TELL 'EM TO WAIT! TELL 'EM IT WAS A MINOR GAS LEAK, BUT WE HAVE IT UNDER CONTROL!
THEY'RE STILL GONNA WANT TO--
THEN STALL 'EM!
I DON'T WANT ANYBODY IN THERE UNTIL I KNOW WHAT THEY'RE GONNA FIND. I HAVE MILLIONS OF DOLLARS IN PLAY OUT ON THE GAMING FLOOR...IF THEY SHUT ME DOWN...
WE HAVE... ANOTHER PROBLEM, SIR.
OH, GOD--WHAT NOW?!
THIS GUY OUT ON THE FLOOR...HE'S BETTING LIKE A LUNATIC.
SO? GOOD!
BUT HE'S WINNING.
"A LOT."
I LOVE THIS GAME!
What's not to love?
IT'S GOT RED, IT'S GOT BLACK, IT'S WILDLY UNPREDICTABLE...
"THAT'S NOT ANOTHER PROBLEM--IT'S THE SAME PROBLEM.
"THAT'S DEADPOOL."

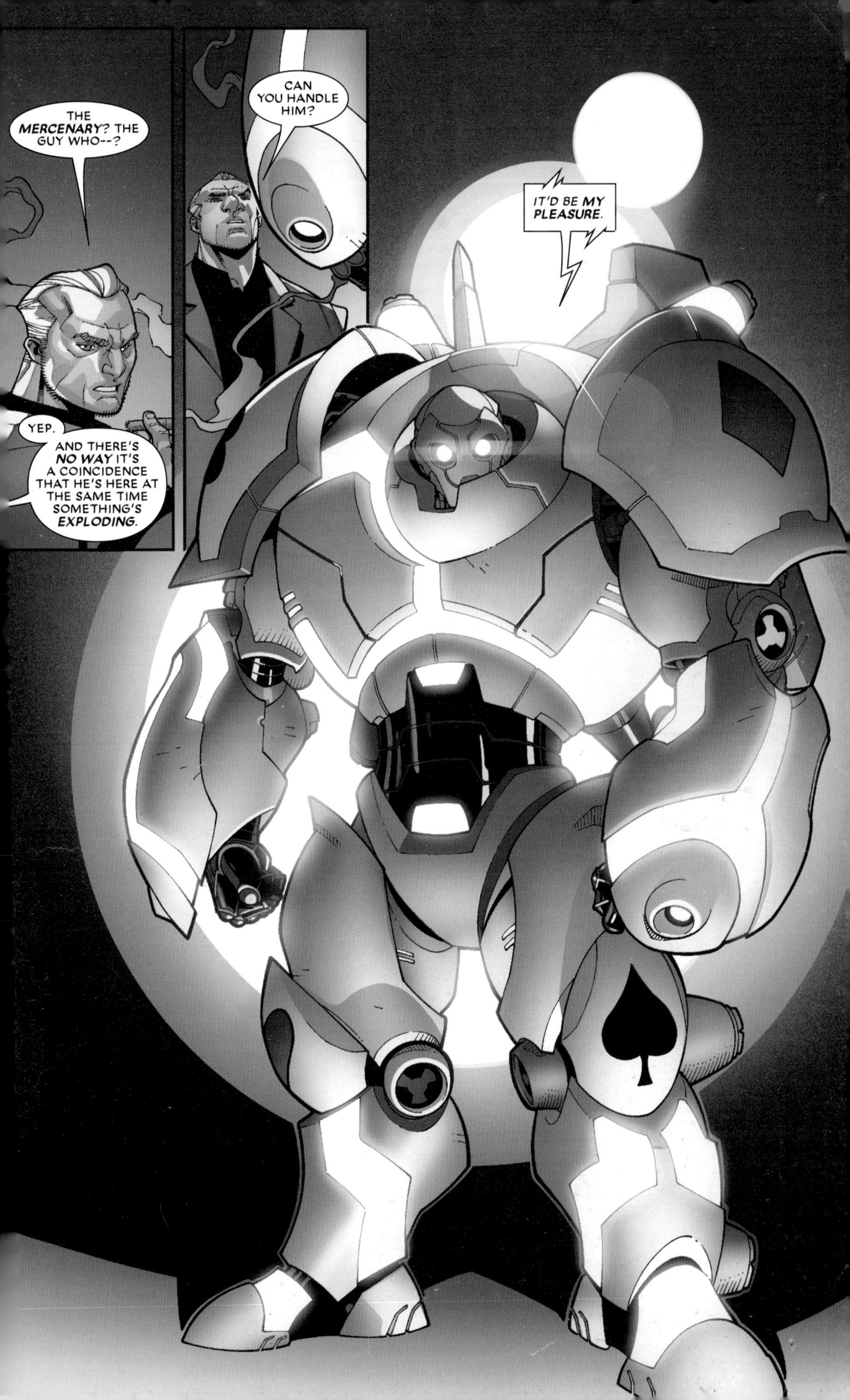
THE *MERCENARY*? THE GUY WHO--?
CAN YOU HANDLE HIM?
YEP.
AND THERE'S *NO WAY* IT'S A COINCIDENCE THAT HE'S HERE AT THE SAME TIME SOMETHING'S *EXPLODING*.
IT'D BE *MY PLEASURE*.

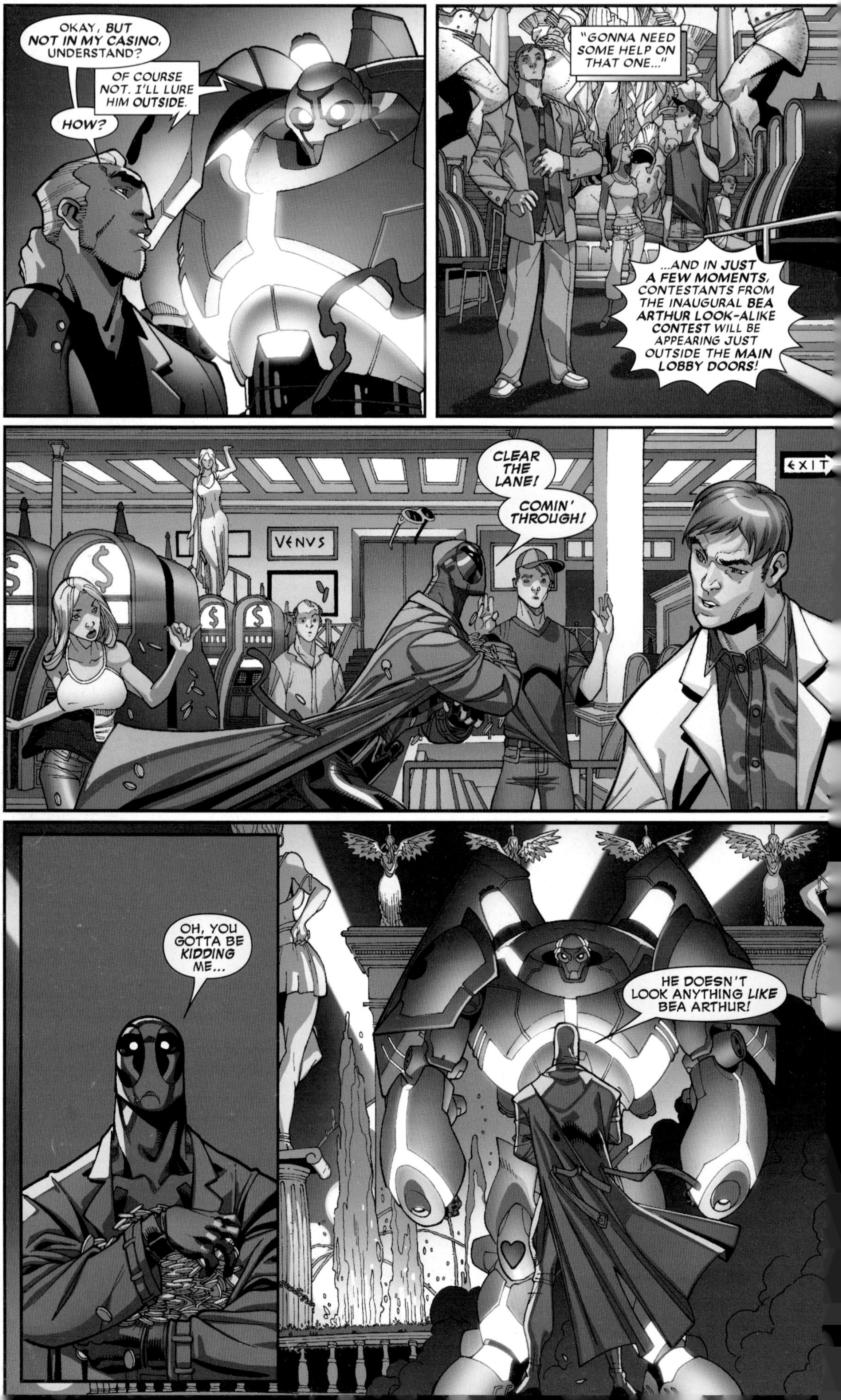
OKAY, BUT NOT IN MY CASINO, UNDERSTAND?
OF COURSE NOT. I'LL LURE HIM OUTSIDE.
HOW?
"GONNA NEED SOME HELP ON THAT ONE..."
...AND IN JUST A FEW MOMENTS, CONTESTANTS FROM THE INAUGURAL BEA ARTHUR LOOK-ALIKE CONTEST WILL BE APPEARING JUST OUTSIDE THE MAIN LOBBY DOORS!
VENUS
EXIT
CLEAR THE LANE!
COMIN' THROUGH!
OH, YOU GOTTA BE KIDDING ME...
HE DOESN'T LOOK ANYTHING LIKE BEA ARTHUR!

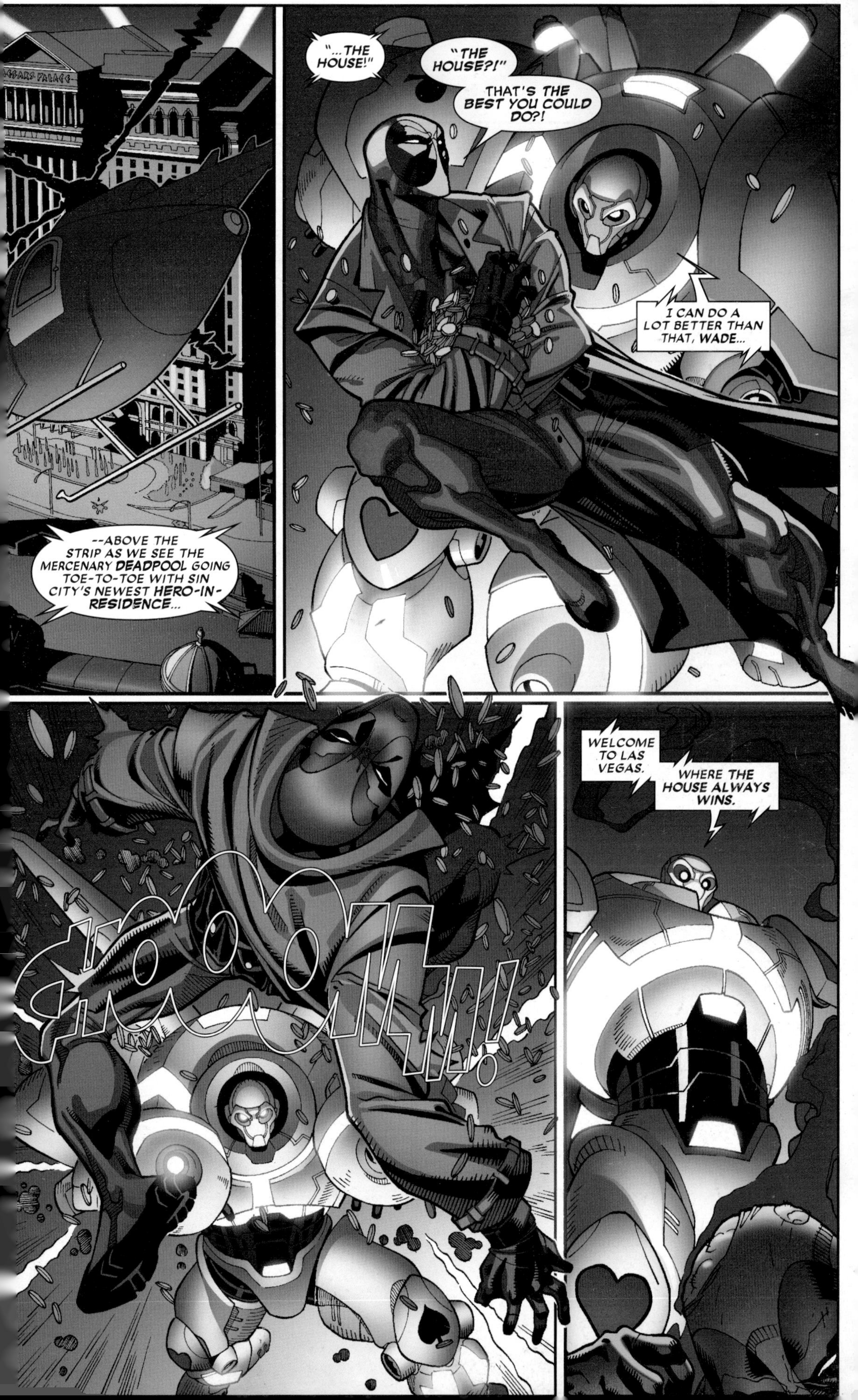
--ABOVE THE STRIP AS WE SEE THE MERCENARY DEADPOOL GOING TOE-TO-TOE WITH SIN CITY'S NEWEST HERO-IN-RESIDENCE...
"...THE HOUSE!"
"THE HOUSE?!"
THAT'S THE BEST YOU COULD DO?!
I CAN DO A LOT BETTER THAN THAT, WADE...
WELCOME TO LAS VEGAS.
WHERE THE HOUSE ALWAYS WINS.

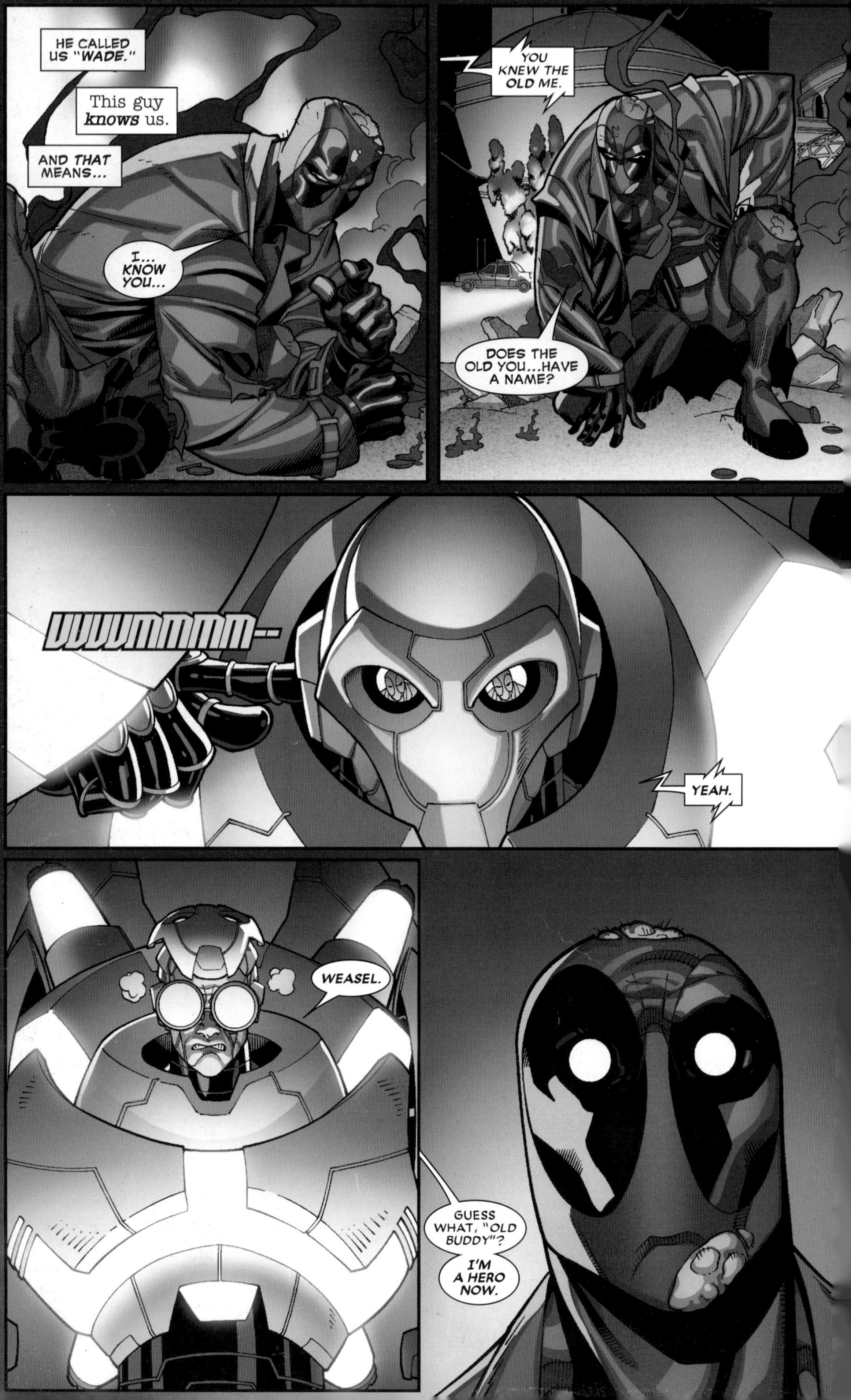
HE CALLED US "WADE."
This guy knows us.
AND THAT MEANS...
I... KNOW YOU...
YOU KNEW THE OLD ME.
DOES THE OLD YOU...HAVE A NAME?
VVVVMMMMM--
YEAH.
WEASEL.
GUESS WHAT, "OLD BUDDY"?
I'M A HERO NOW.

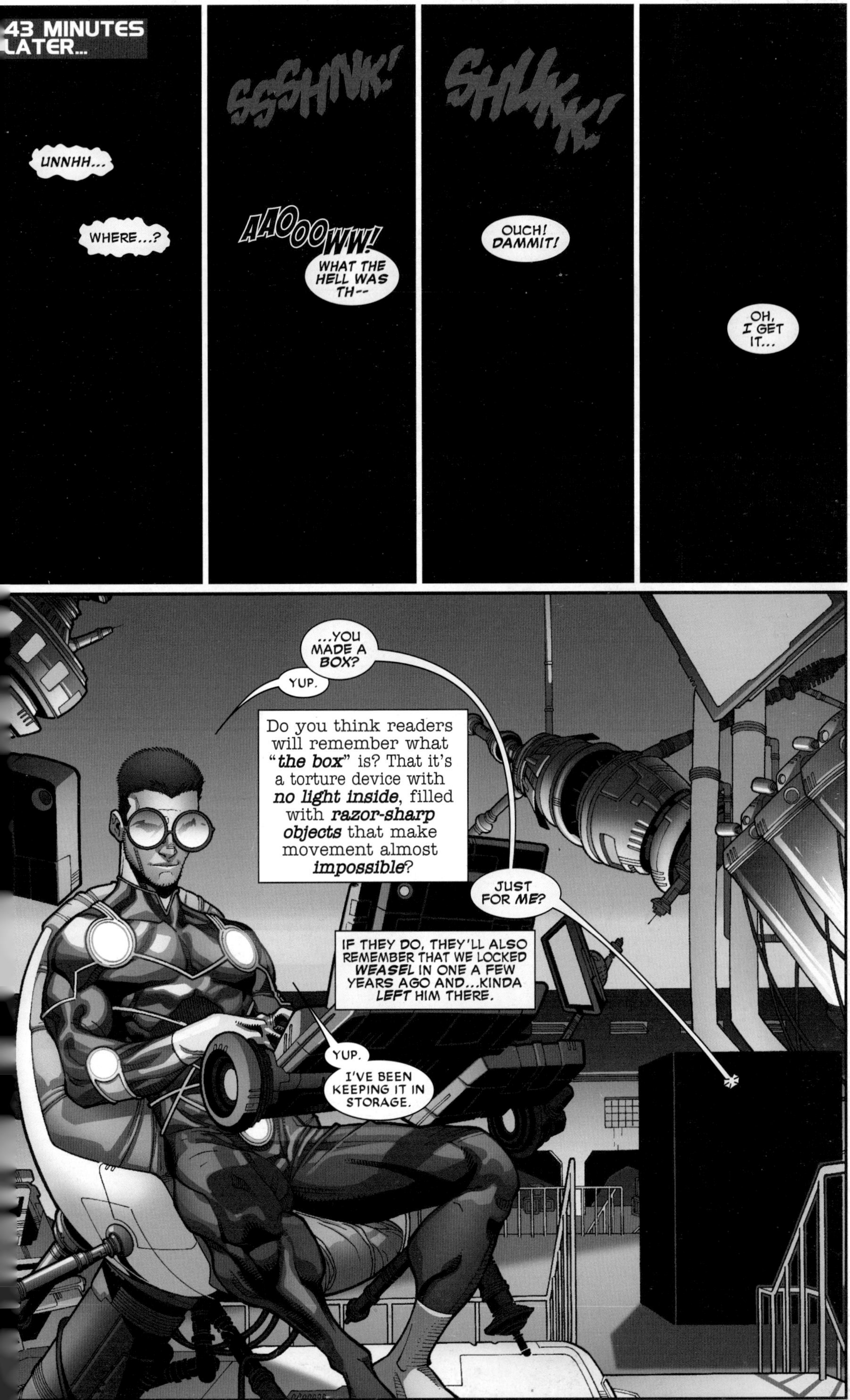
43 MINUTES LATER...
UNNHH...
WHERE...?
SSSHINK!
AAOOOOWW!
WHAT THE HELL WAS TH--
SHUKK!
OUCH! DAMMIT!
OH, I GET IT...
...YOU MADE A BOX?
YUP.
Do you think readers will remember what "the box" is? That it's a torture device with no light inside, filled with razor-sharp objects that make movement almost impossible?
JUST FOR ME?
IF THEY DO, THEY'LL ALSO REMEMBER THAT WE LOCKED WEASEL IN ONE A FEW YEARS AGO AND...KINDA LEFT HIM THERE.
YUP.
I'VE BEEN KEEPING IT IN STORAGE.

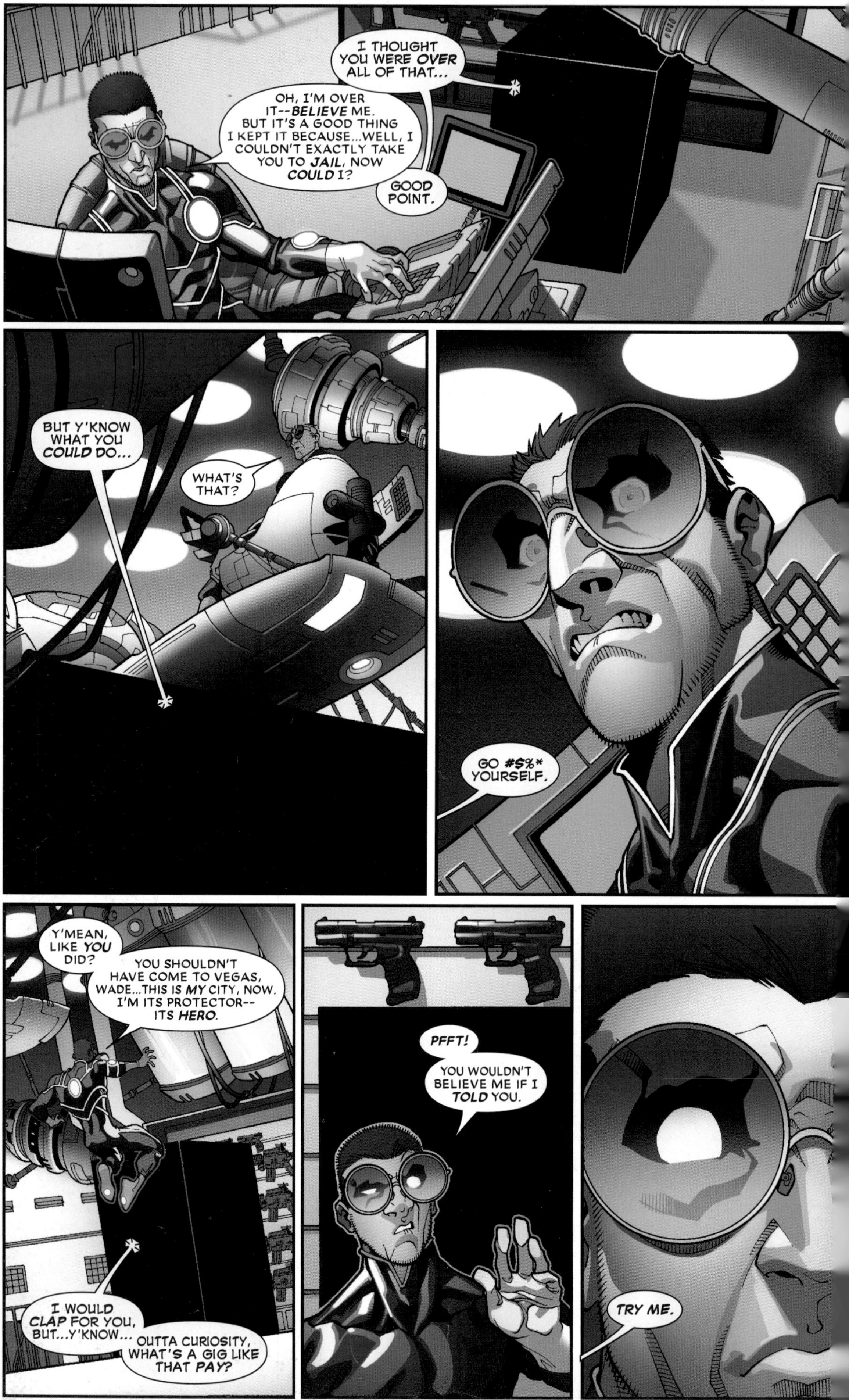
I THOUGHT YOU WERE OVER ALL OF THAT...
OH, I'M OVER IT--BELIEVE ME. BUT IT'S A GOOD THING I KEPT IT BECAUSE...WELL, I COULDN'T EXACTLY TAKE YOU TO JAIL, NOW COULD I?
GOOD POINT.
BUT Y'KNOW WHAT YOU COULD DO...
WHAT'S THAT?
GO #$%* YOURSELF.
Y'MEAN, LIKE YOU DID?
YOU SHOULDN'T HAVE COME TO VEGAS, WADE...THIS IS MY CITY, NOW. I'M ITS PROTECTOR-- ITS HERO.
I WOULD CLAP FOR YOU, BUT...Y'KNOW...
OUTTA CURIOSITY, WHAT'S A GIG LIKE THAT PAY?
PFFT!
YOU WOULDN'T BELIEVE ME IF I TOLD YOU.
TRY ME.

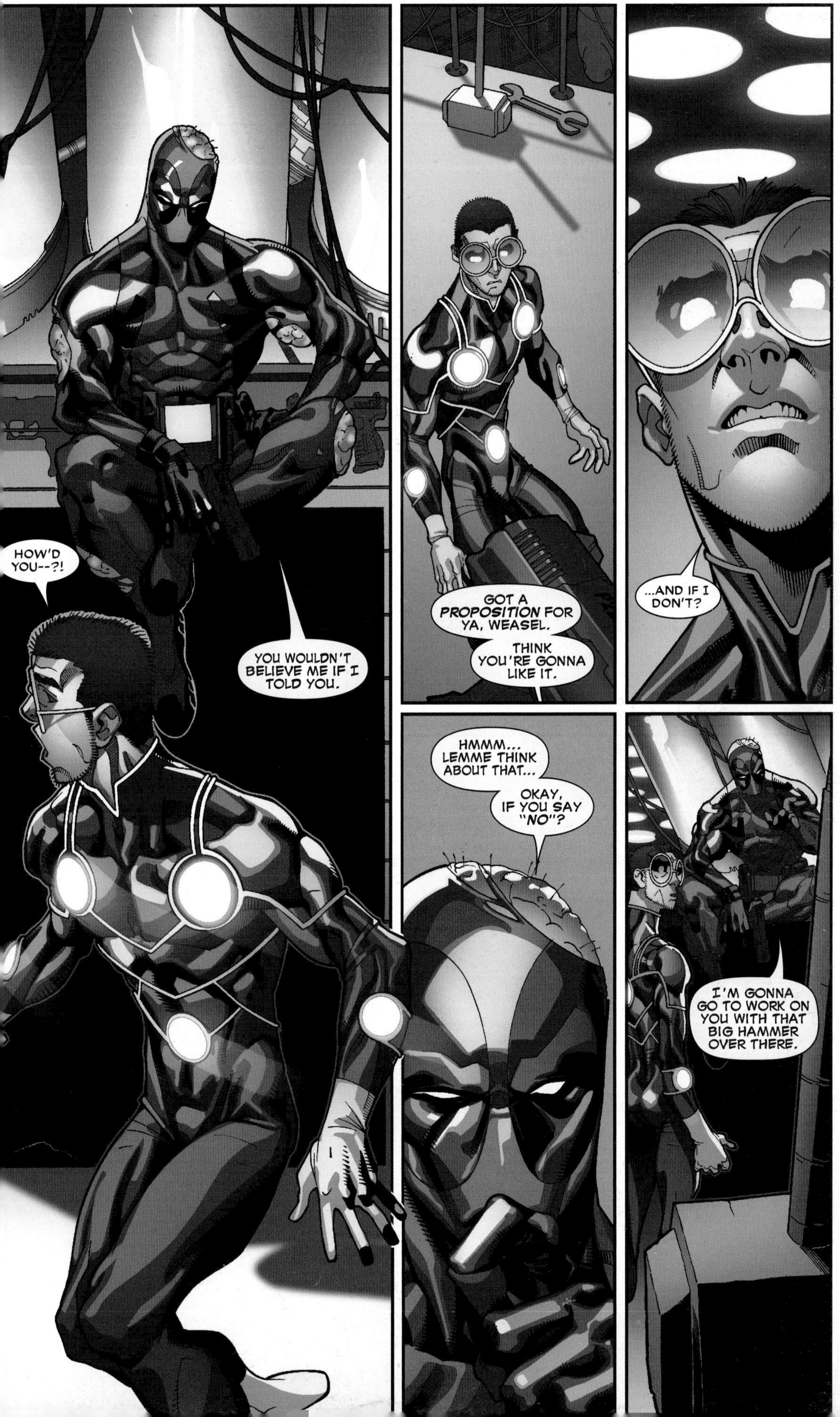
HOW'D YOU--?!
YOU WOULDN'T BELIEVE ME IF I TOLD YOU.
GOT A *PROPOSITION* FOR YA, WEASEL.
THINK YOU'RE GONNA LIKE IT.
...AND IF I DON'T?
HMMM... LEMME THINK ABOUT THAT...
OKAY, IF YOU SAY "*NO*"?
I'M GONNA GO TO WORK ON YOU WITH THAT BIG HAMMER OVER THERE.

BUT IF YOU SAY "YES"?

YOU'LL BE MAKIN' TWICE AS MUCH AS YOU ARE NOW.

BUT... HOW?

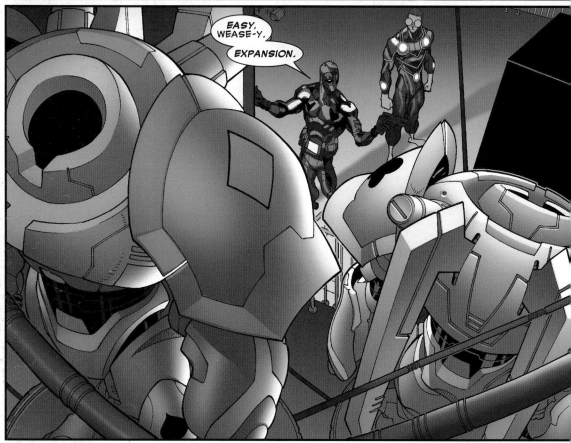

EASY, WEASE-Y.

EXPANSION.

YOU GOT TWO OF THESE THINGS... MIGHT AS WELL USE 'EM, RIGHT?

Y'MEAN... YOU?

I MEAN US. PARTNER.

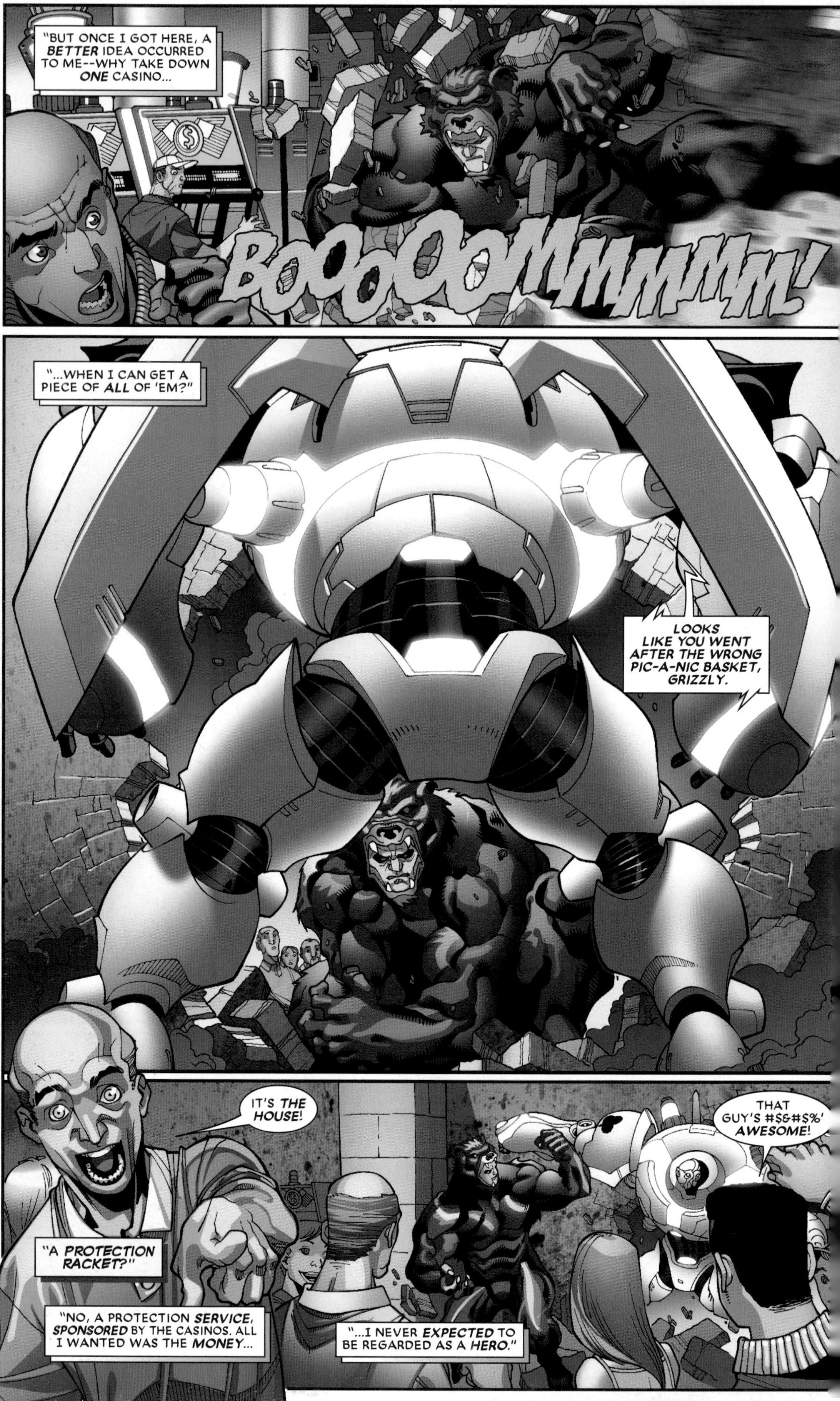
"BUT ONCE I GOT HERE, A BETTER IDEA OCCURRED TO ME--WHY TAKE DOWN ONE CASINO...
BOOOOOMMMMMM!
"...WHEN I CAN GET A PIECE OF ALL OF 'EM?"
LOOKS LIKE YOU WENT AFTER THE WRONG PIC-A-NIC BASKET, GRIZZLY.
IT'S THE HOUSE!
THAT GUY'S #$&#$%' AWESOME!
"A PROTECTION RACKET?"
"NO, A PROTECTION SERVICE, SPONSORED BY THE CASINOS. ALL I WANTED WAS THE MONEY...
"...I NEVER EXPECTED TO BE REGARDED AS A HERO."

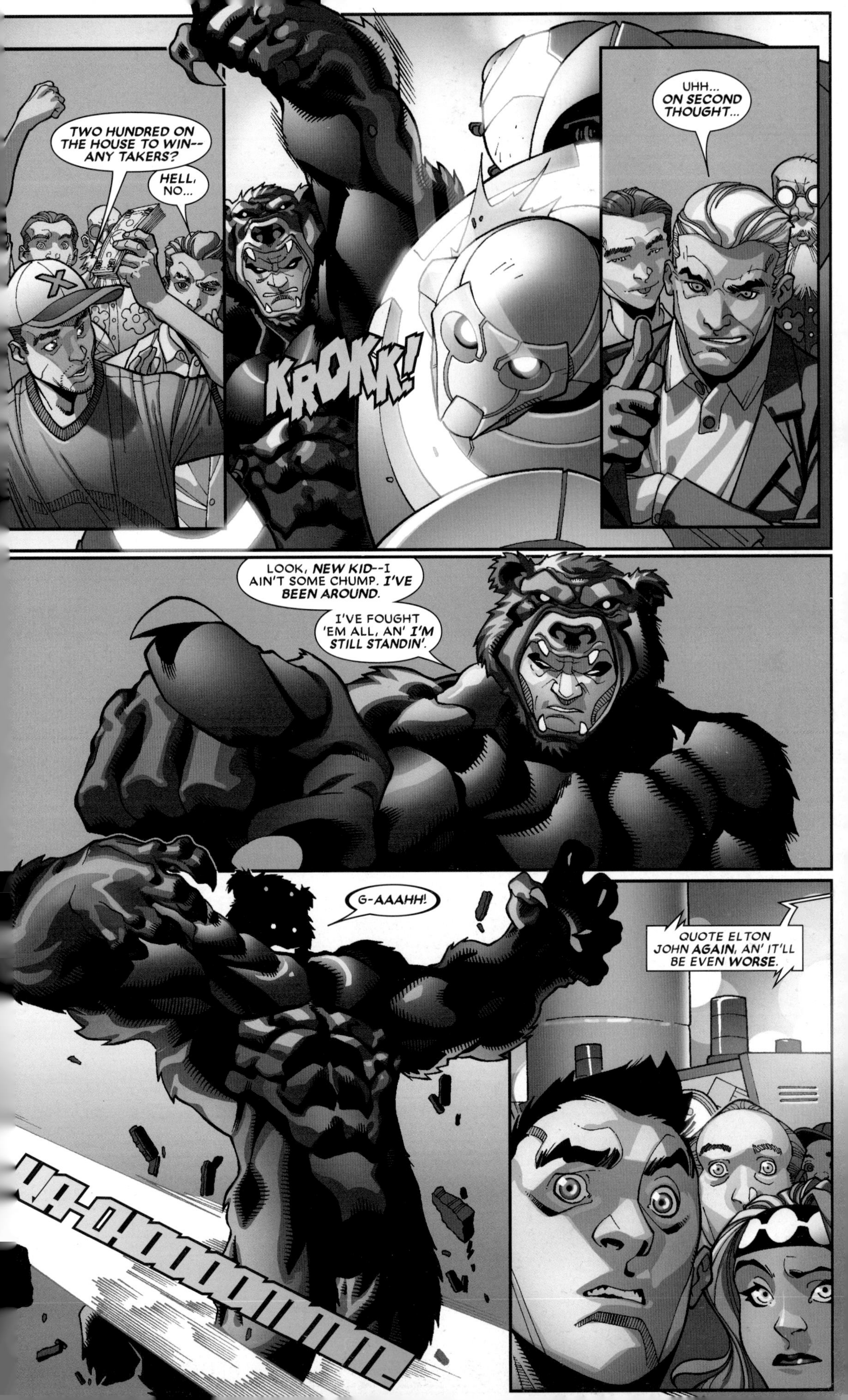
TWO HUNDRED ON THE HOUSE TO WIN-- ANY TAKERS?
HELL, NO...
KROKK!
UHH... ON SECOND THOUGHT...
LOOK, NEW KID--I AIN'T SOME CHUMP. I'VE BEEN AROUND.
I'VE FOUGHT 'EM ALL, AN' I'M STILL STANDIN'.
G-AAAHH!
QUOTE ELTON JOHN AGAIN, AN' IT'LL BE EVEN WORSE.

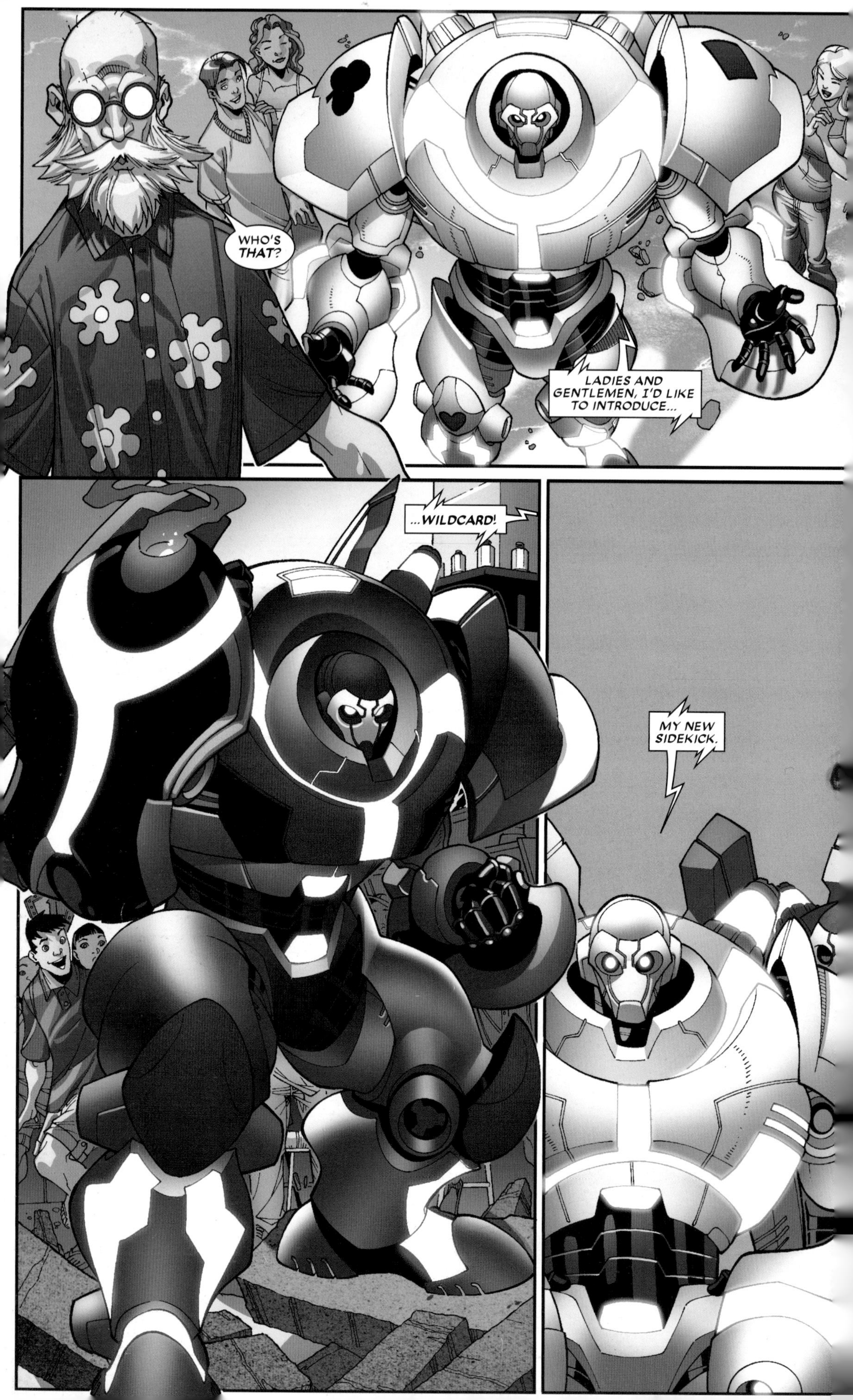
WHO'S THAT?
LADIES AND GENTLEMEN, I'D LIKE TO INTRODUCE...
...WILDCARD!
MY NEW SIDEKICK.

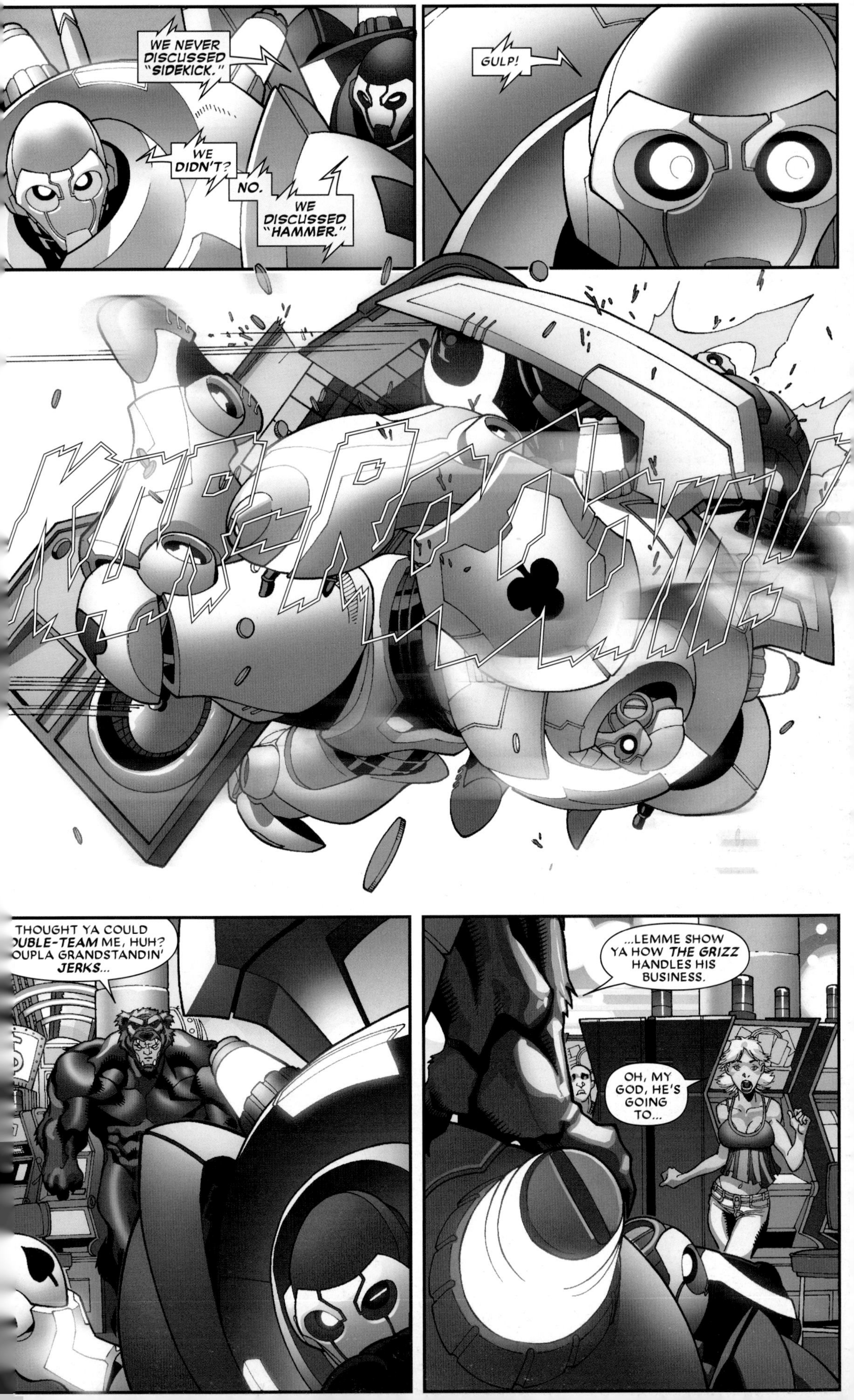

WE NEVER DISCUSSED "SIDEKICK."
WE DIDN'T?
NO.
WE DISCUSSED "HAMMER."
GULP!
THOUGHT YA COULD OUBLE-TEAM ME, HUH? OUPLA GRANDSTANDIN' JERKS...
...LEMME SHOW YA HOW THE GRIZZ HANDLES HIS BUSINESS.
OH, MY GOD, HE'S GOING TO...

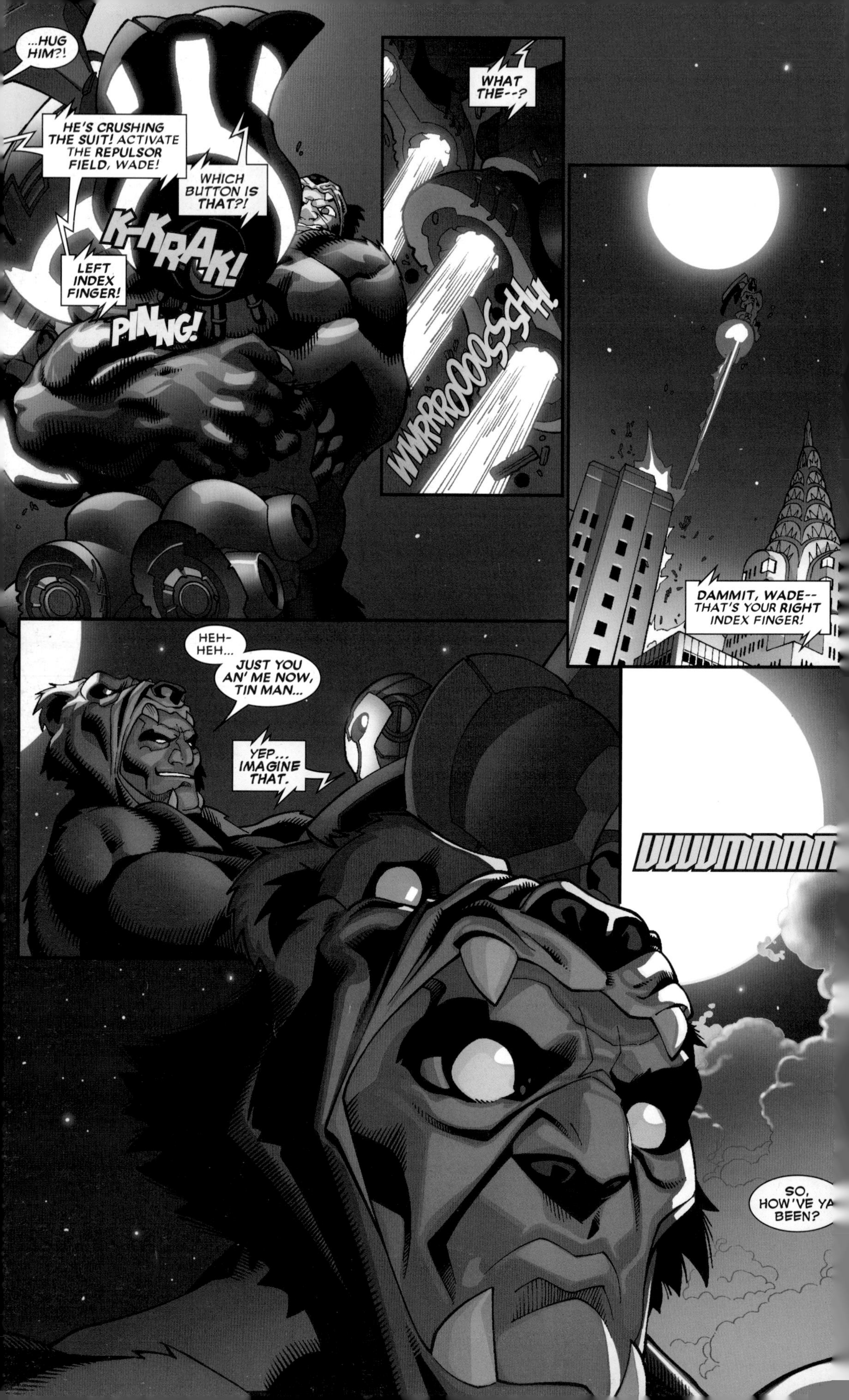
...HUG HIM?!
HE'S CRUSHING THE SUIT! ACTIVATE THE REPULSOR FIELD, WADE!
WHICH BUTTON IS THAT?!
K-KRAK!
LEFT INDEX FINGER!
PINNG!
WHAT THE--?
WWRRROOOOSSCH!
DAMMIT, WADE-- THAT'S YOUR RIGHT INDEX FINGER!
HEH-HEH...
JUST YOU AN' ME NOW, TIN MAN...
YEP... IMAGINE THAT.
VVVVMMMMM
SO, HOW'VE YA BEEN?

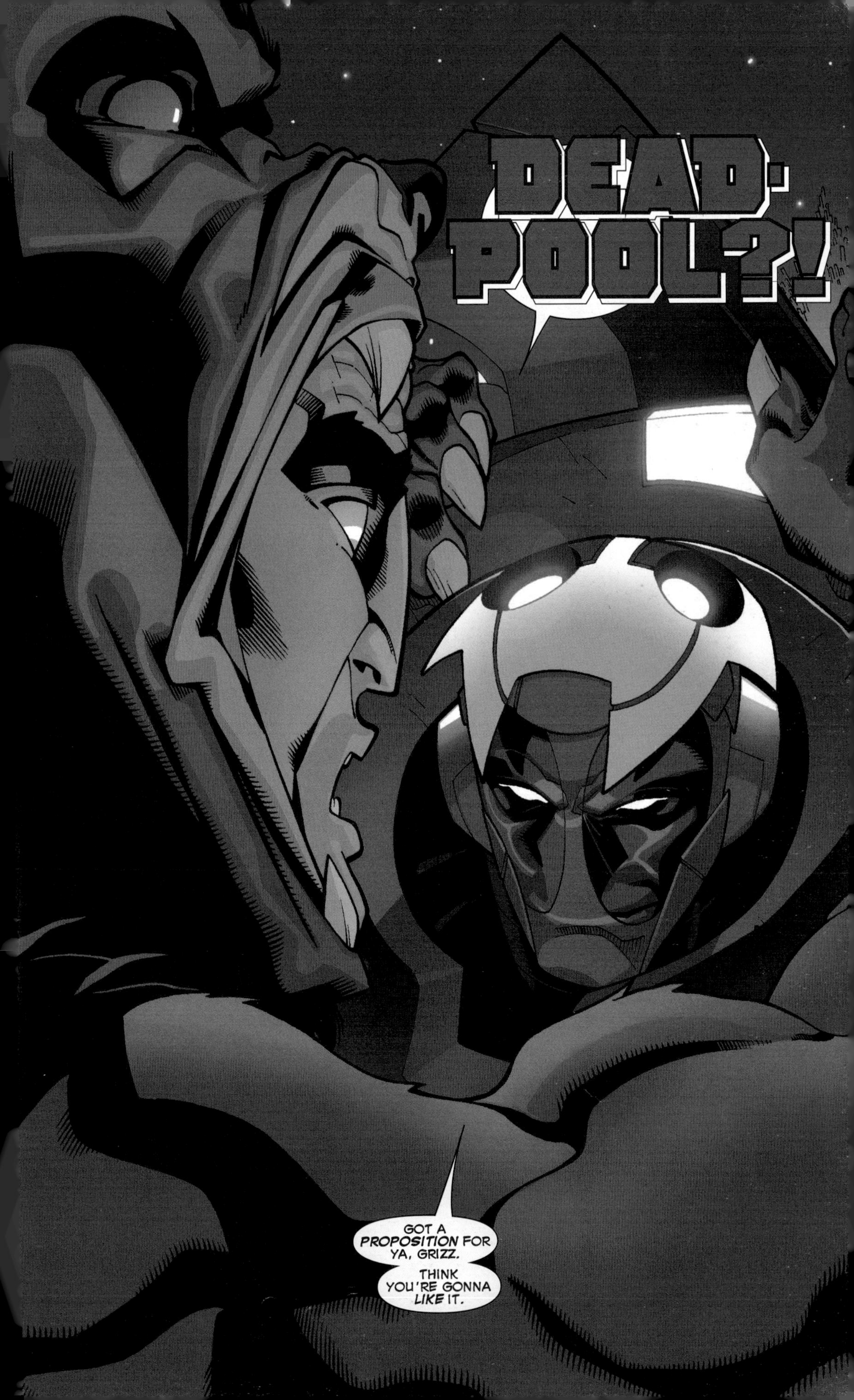
DEAD-POOL?!
GOT A *PROPOSITION* FOR YA, GRIZZ.
THINK YOU'RE GONNA *LIKE* IT.

24

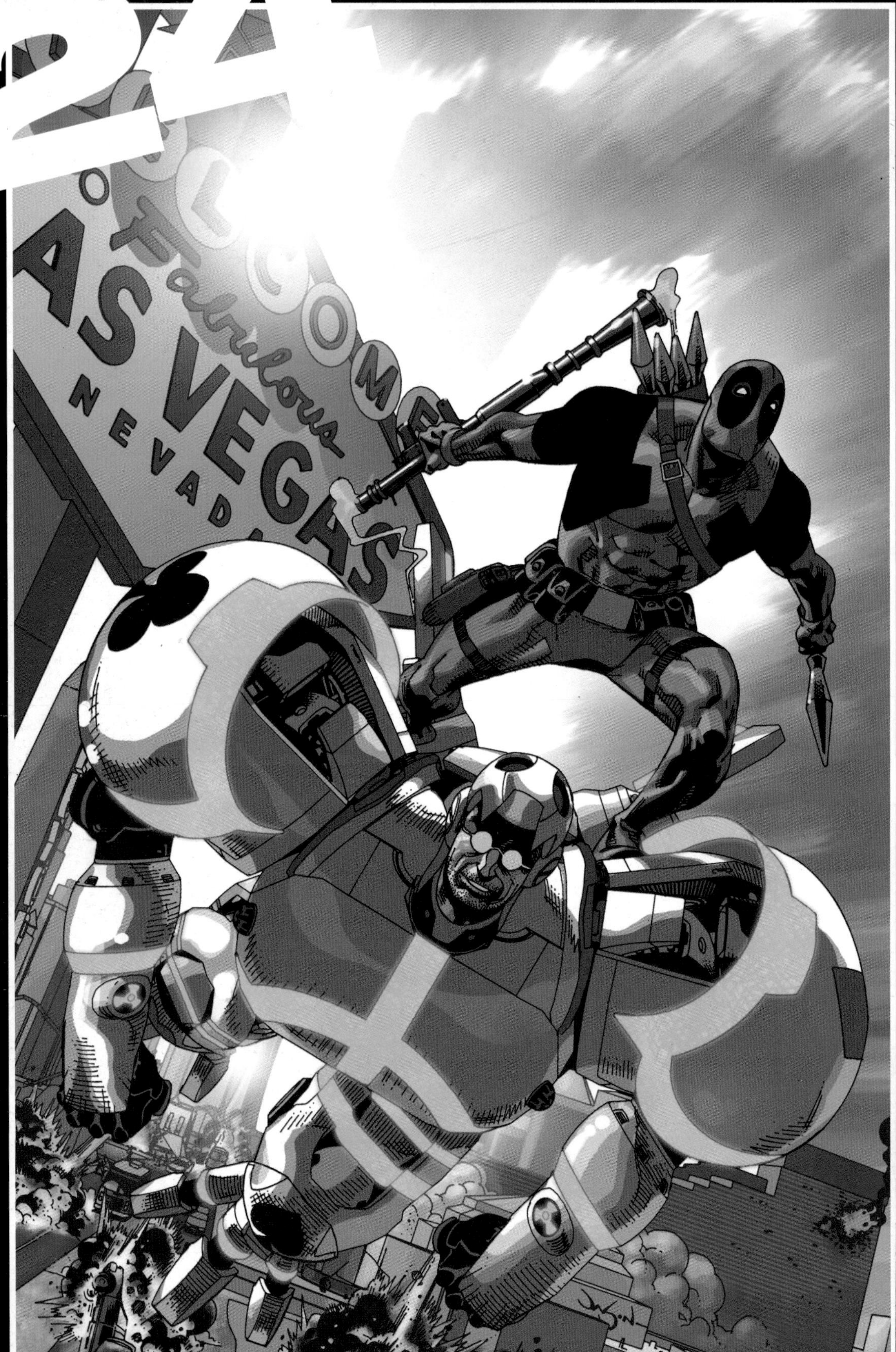
Fabulous

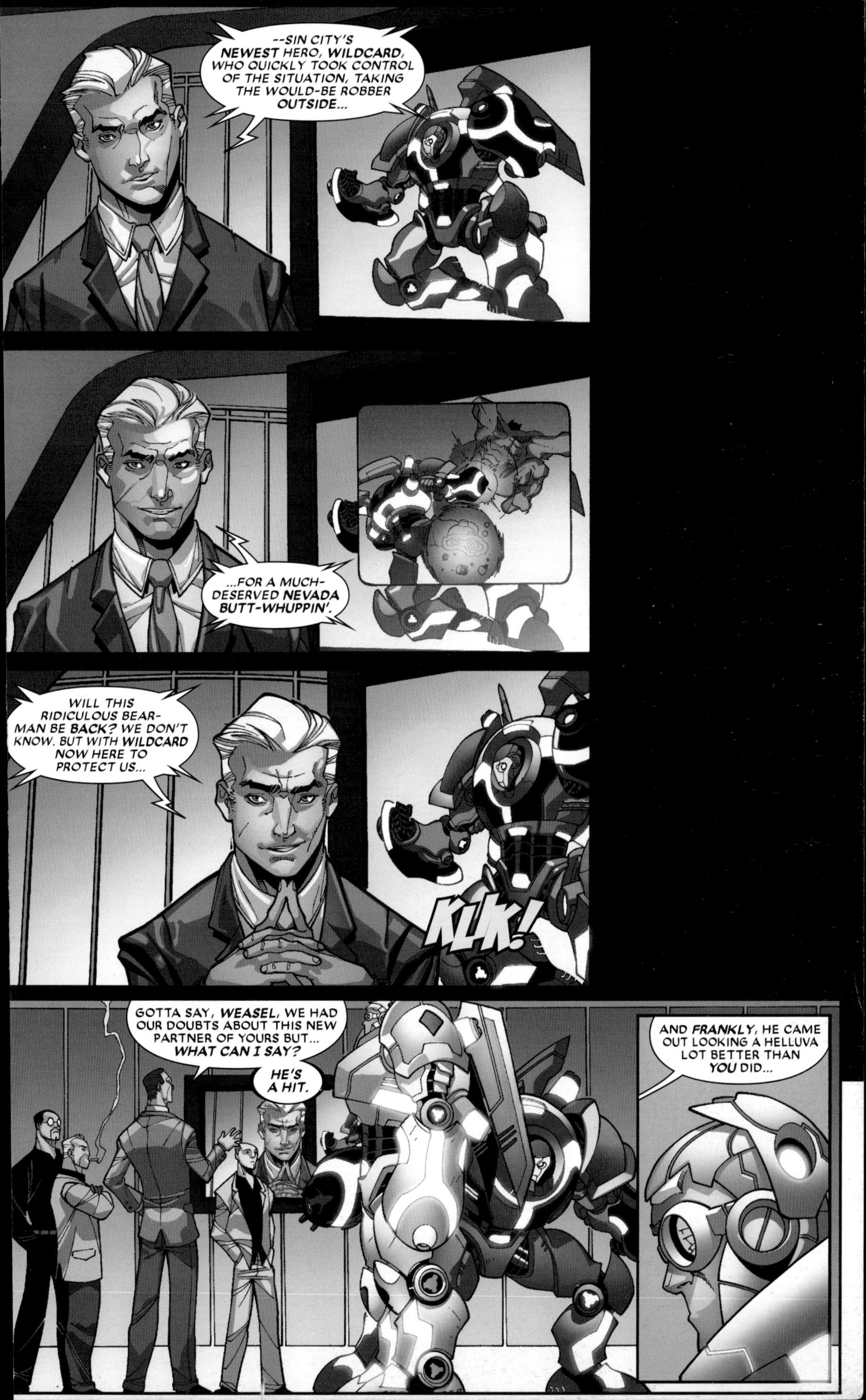
--SIN CITY'S NEWEST HERO, WILDCARD, WHO QUICKLY TOOK CONTROL OF THE SITUATION, TAKING THE WOULD-BE ROBBER OUTSIDE...
...FOR A MUCH-DESERVED NEVADA BUTT-WHUPPIN'.
WILL THIS RIDICULOUS BEAR-MAN BE BACK? WE DON'T KNOW. BUT WITH WILDCARD NOW HERE TO PROTECT US...
KLIK!
GOTTA SAY, WEASEL, WE HAD OUR DOUBTS ABOUT THIS NEW PARTNER OF YOURS BUT... WHAT CAN I SAY?
HE'S A HIT.
AND FRANKLY, HE CAME OUT LOOKING A HELLUVA LOT BETTER THAN YOU DID...

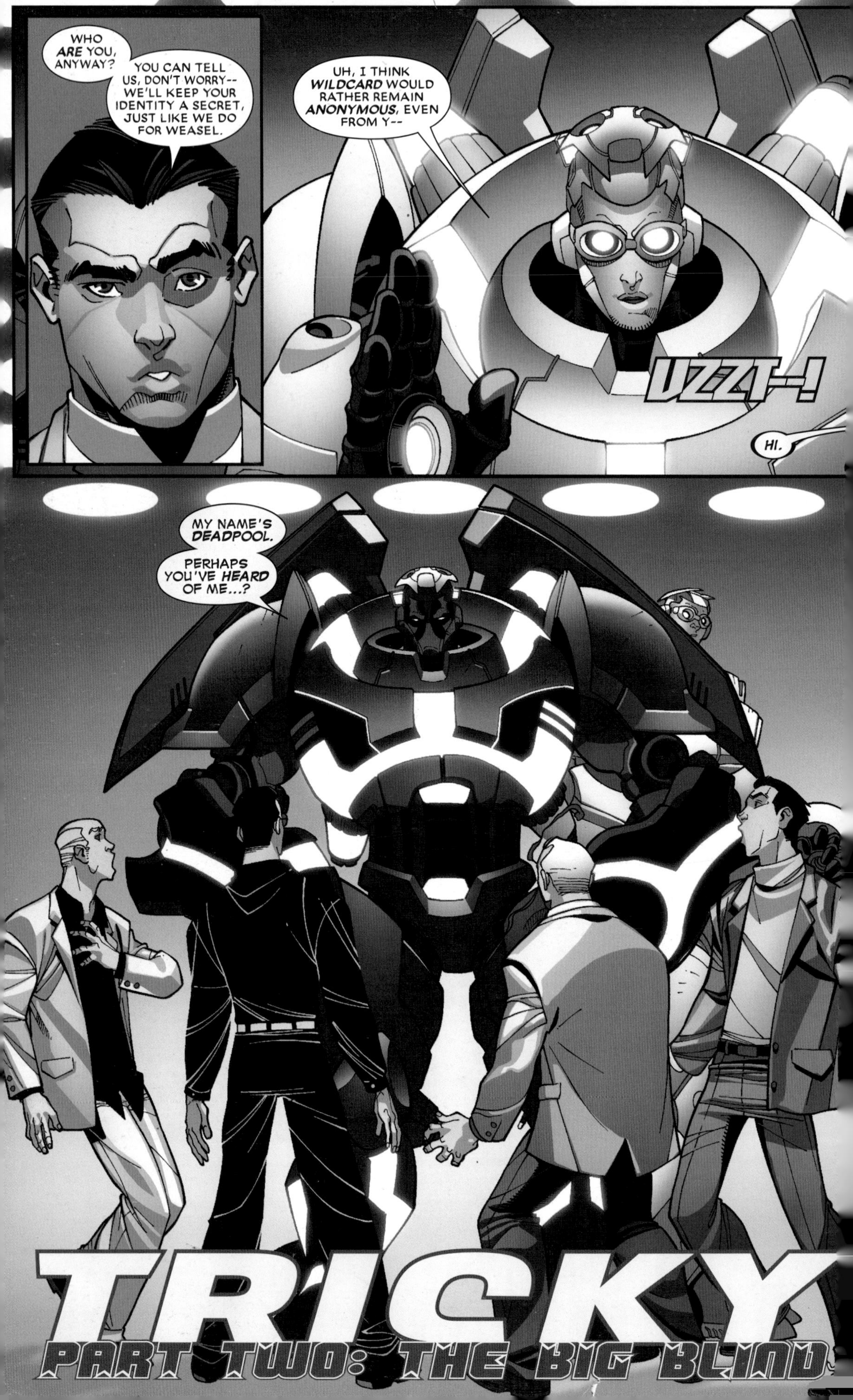

WHO ARE YOU, ANYWAY?
YOU CAN TELL US, DON'T WORRY-- WE'LL KEEP YOUR IDENTITY A SECRET, JUST LIKE WE DO FOR WEASEL.
UH, I THINK WILDCARD WOULD RATHER REMAIN ANONYMOUS, EVEN FROM Y--
VZZT--!
HI.
MY NAME'S DEADPOOL.
PERHAPS YOU'VE HEARD OF ME...?
TRICKY
PART TWO: THE BIG BLIND

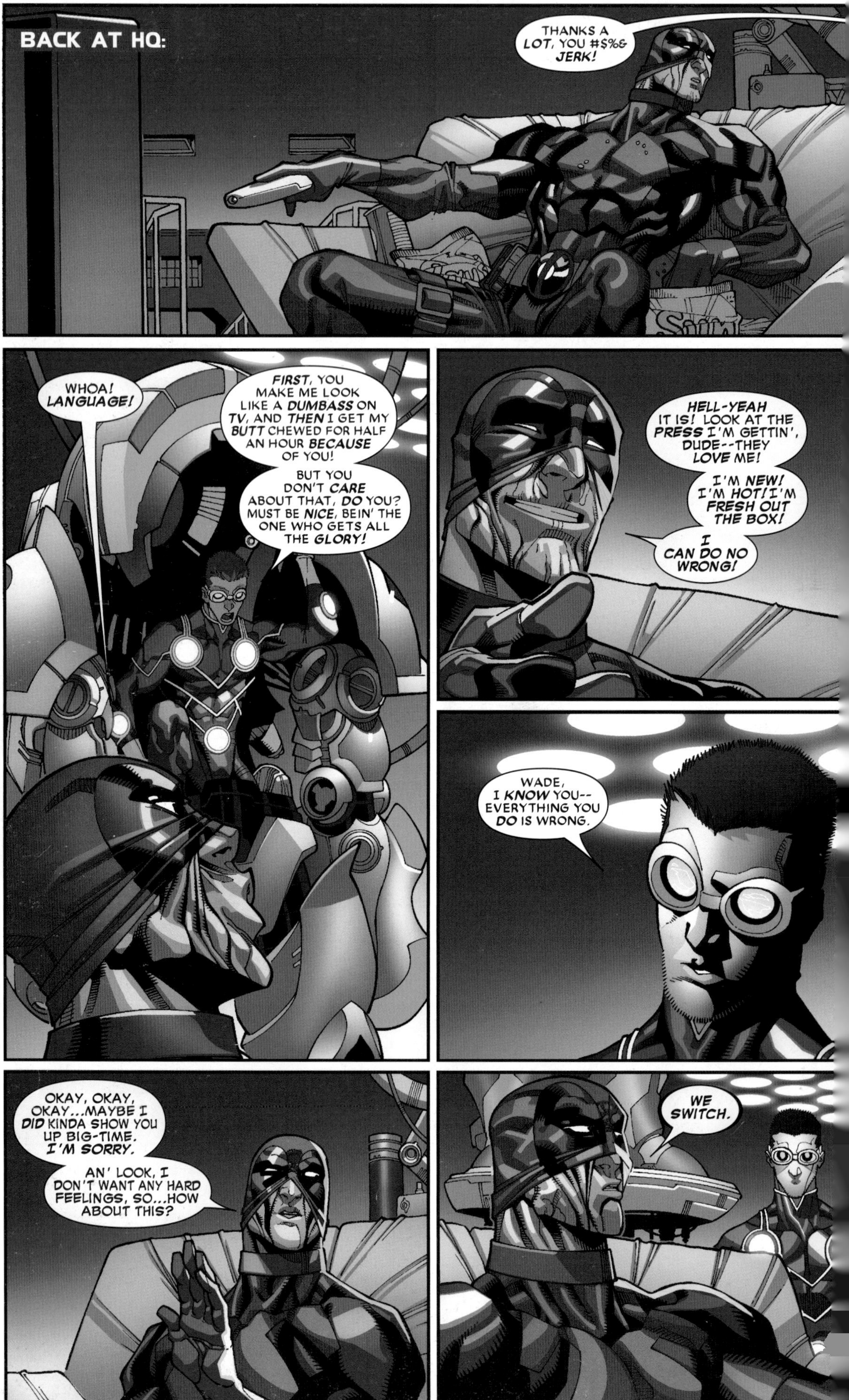
BACK AT HQ:
THANKS A LOT, YOU #$%& JERK!
WHOA! LANGUAGE!
FIRST, YOU MAKE ME LOOK LIKE A DUMBASS ON TV, AND THEN I GET MY BUTT CHEWED FOR HALF AN HOUR BECAUSE OF YOU!
BUT YOU DON'T CARE ABOUT THAT, DO YOU? MUST BE NICE, BEIN' THE ONE WHO GETS ALL THE GLORY!
HELL-YEAH IT IS! LOOK AT THE PRESS I'M GETTIN', DUDE--THEY LOVE ME!
I'M NEW! I'M HOT! I'M FRESH OUT THE BOX!
I CAN DO NO WRONG!
WADE, I KNOW YOU--EVERYTHING YOU DO IS WRONG.
OKAY, OKAY, OKAY...MAYBE I DID KINDA SHOW YOU UP BIG-TIME. I'M SORRY.
AN' LOOK, I DON'T WANT ANY HARD FEELINGS, SO...HOW ABOUT THIS?
WE SWITCH.

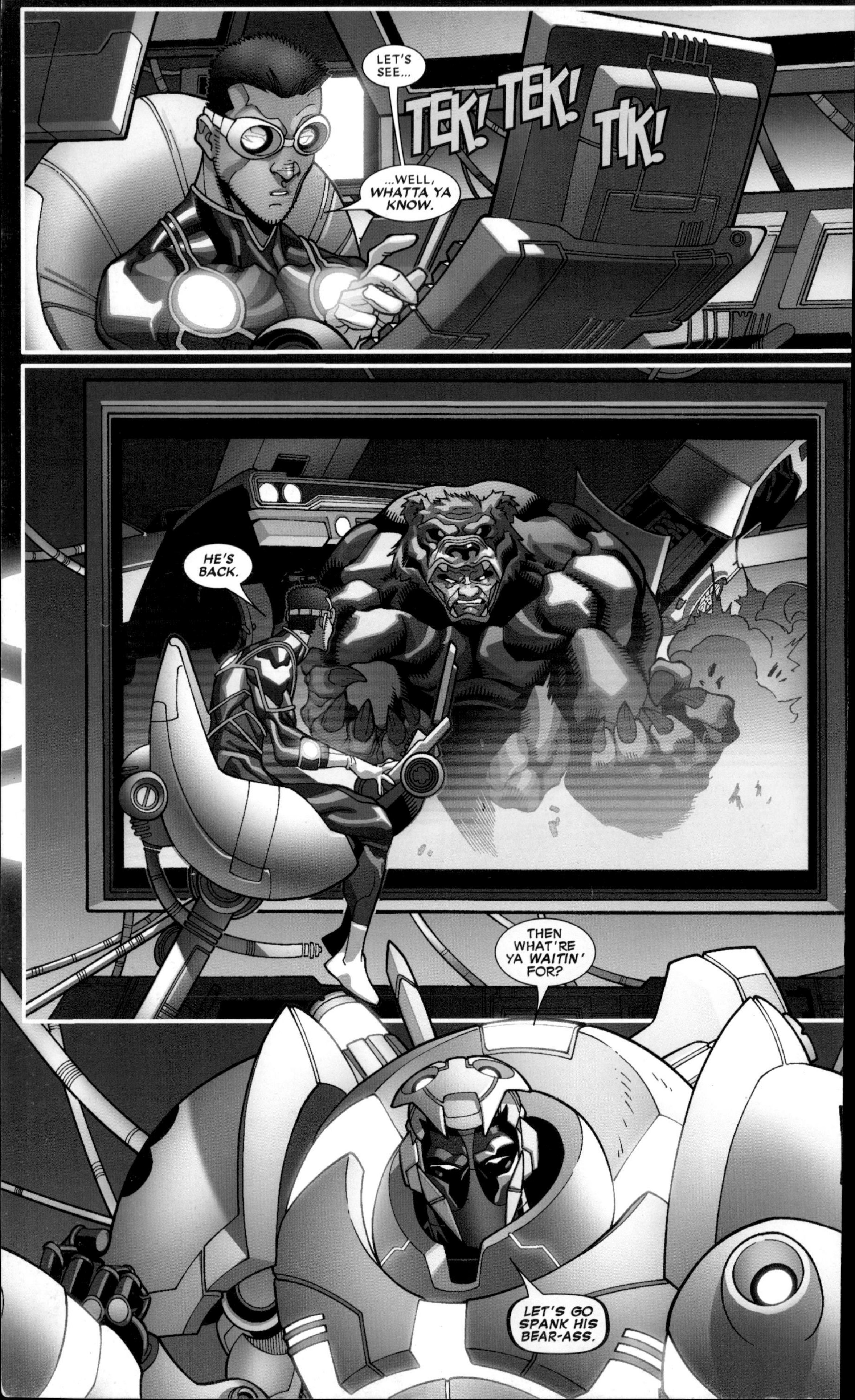
LET'S SEE...
TEK! TEK! TIK!
...WELL, WHATTA YA KNOW.
HE'S BACK.
THEN WHAT'RE YA WAITIN' FOR?
LET'S GO SPANK HIS BEAR-ASS.

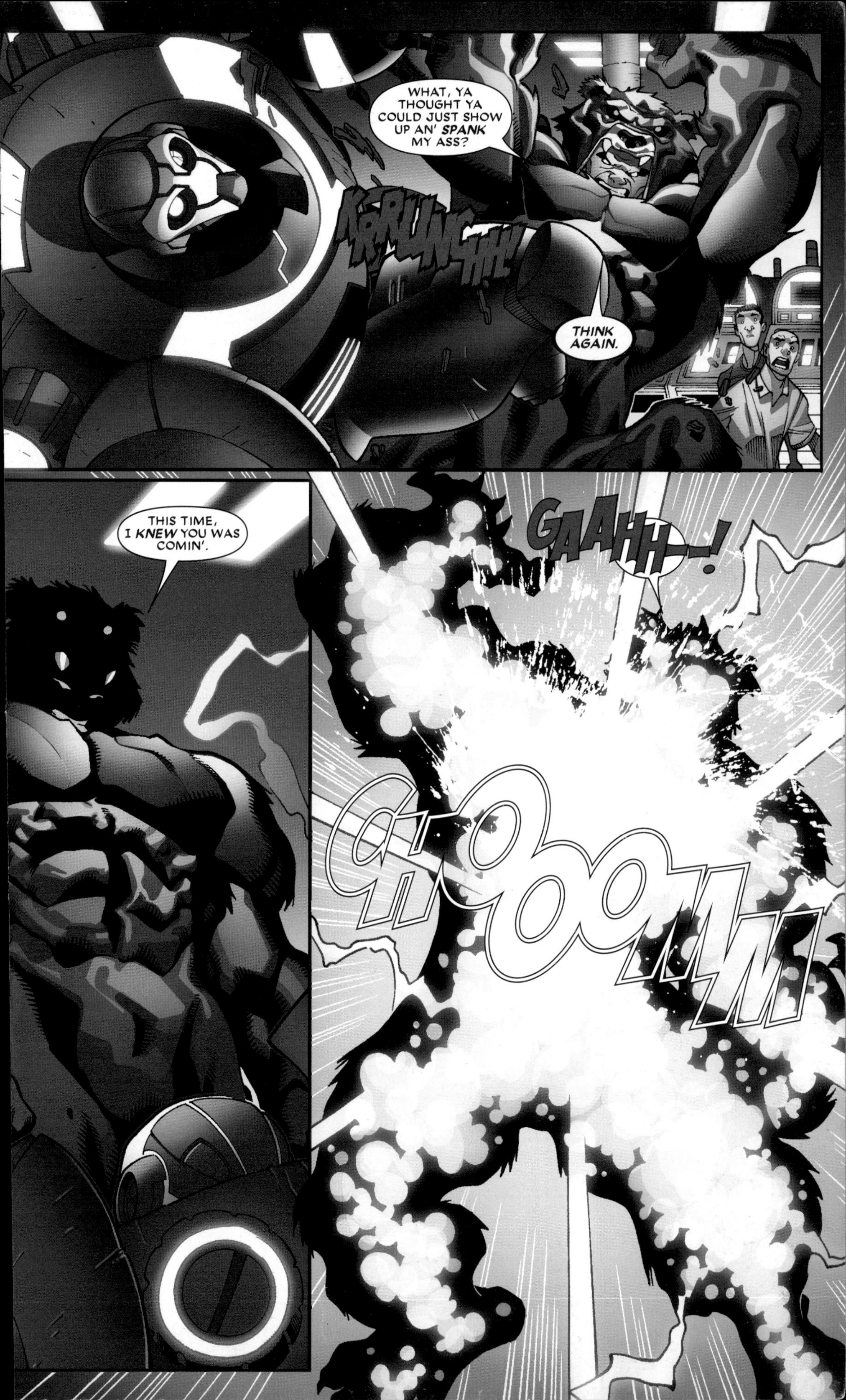
WHAT, YA THOUGHT YA COULD JUST SHOW UP AN' SPANK MY ASS?
KRUNCHH!
THINK AGAIN.
THIS TIME, I KNEW YOU WAS COMIN'.
GAAHH--!
CHOOOMM

YOU BACK-SHOOTIN' SON OF A--

AH-AH-AH...

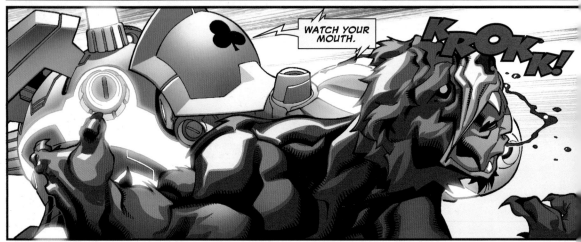

WATCH YOUR MOUTH.

KROKK!

DUDE, GET UP! YOU'RE MAKIN' ME LOOK BAD!

DON'T WORRY ABOUT ME--!

I'M NOT! I'M WORRIED ABOUT ME... THE OL' SWITCHEROO, REMEMBER? I CAN'T HAVE PEOPLE THINKIN' THAT--

DAMMIT, HE'S GETTING AWAY!

RUNNING AWAY IS MORE LIKE IT...

HE'S HEADED FOR THE COUNTING ROOM!

C'MON!

THE WHAAA--?!

THE COUNTING ROOM, YOU IDIOT!

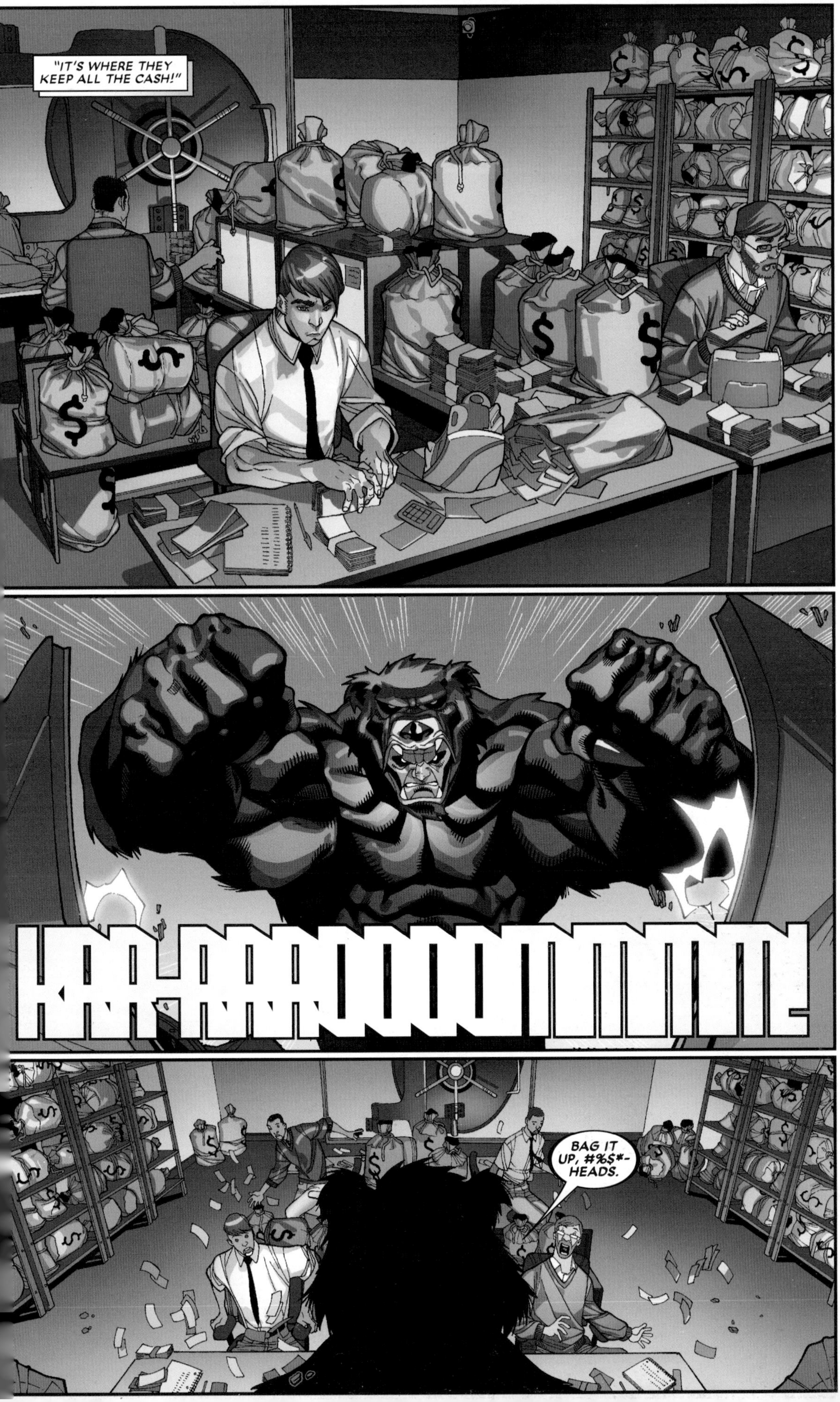
"IT'S WHERE THEY KEEP ALL THE CASH!"
KA-AAAROOOOMMME!
BAG IT UP, #%$*-HEADS.

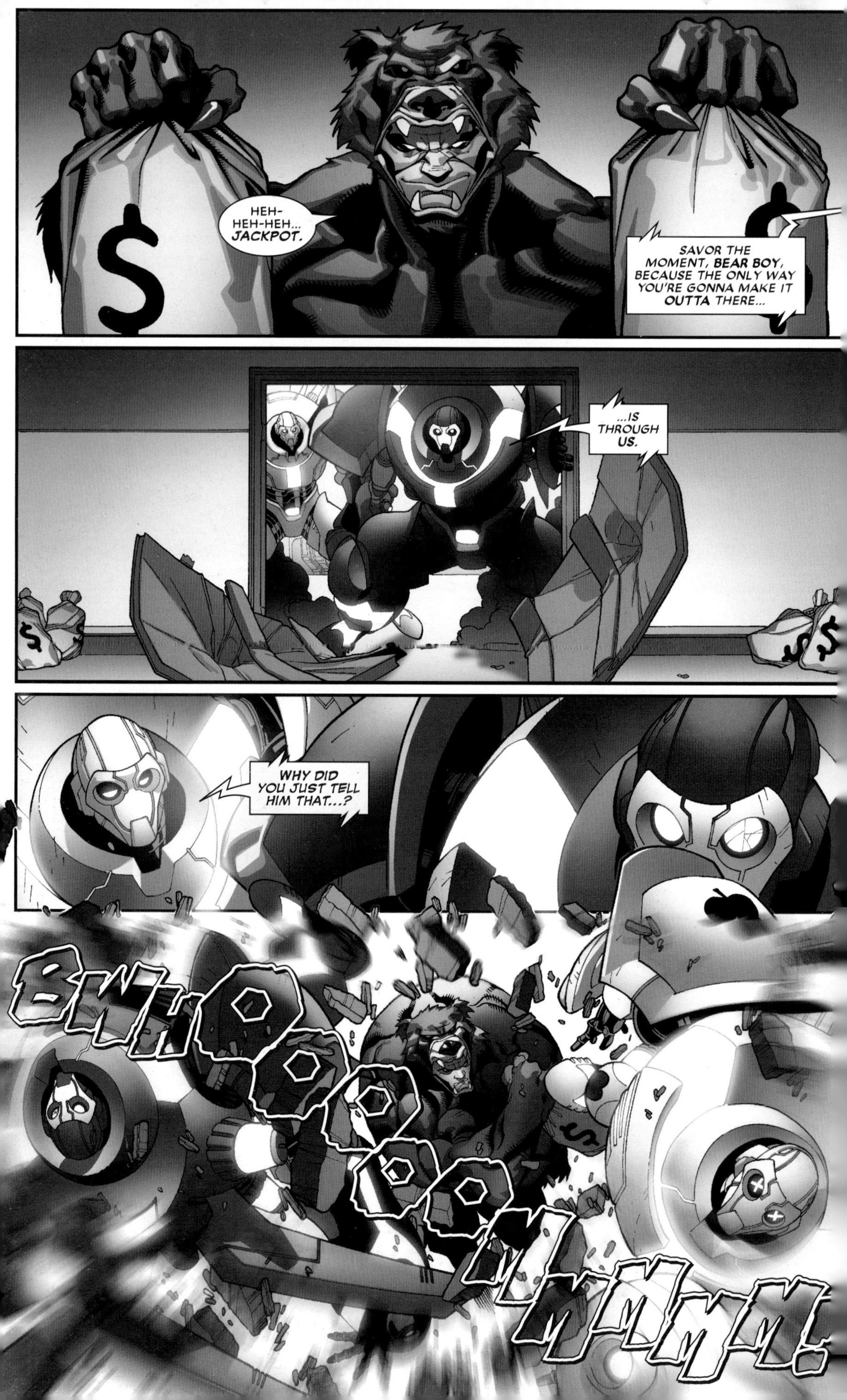
HEH-
HEH-HEH...
JACKPOT.
SAVOR THE MOMENT, BEAR BOY, BECAUSE THE ONLY WAY YOU'RE GONNA MAKE IT OUTTA THERE...
...IS THROUGH US.
WHY DID YOU JUST TELL HIM THAT...?
BWHOOOOOOMMMMM!

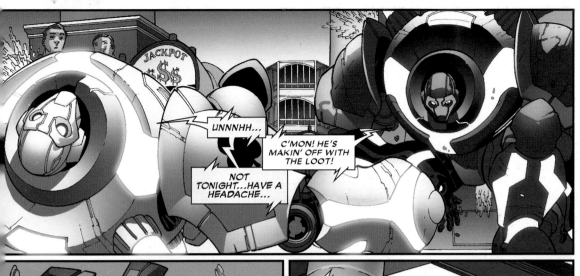

UNNNHH...

C'MON! HE'S MAKIN' OFF WITH THE LOOT!

NOT TONIGHT...HAVE A HEADACHE...

YOU'RE GIVING UP?!

YOU SHOULD BE ASHAMED OF YOURSELF.

Y'know what?

WE KINDA ARE.

WHY DO THEY MAKE IT SO HARD TO GET OUTTA THESE FRICKIN' PLACES?!

OUTTA THE WAY, SUCKERS!

LEMME HELP YOU WITH THAT...

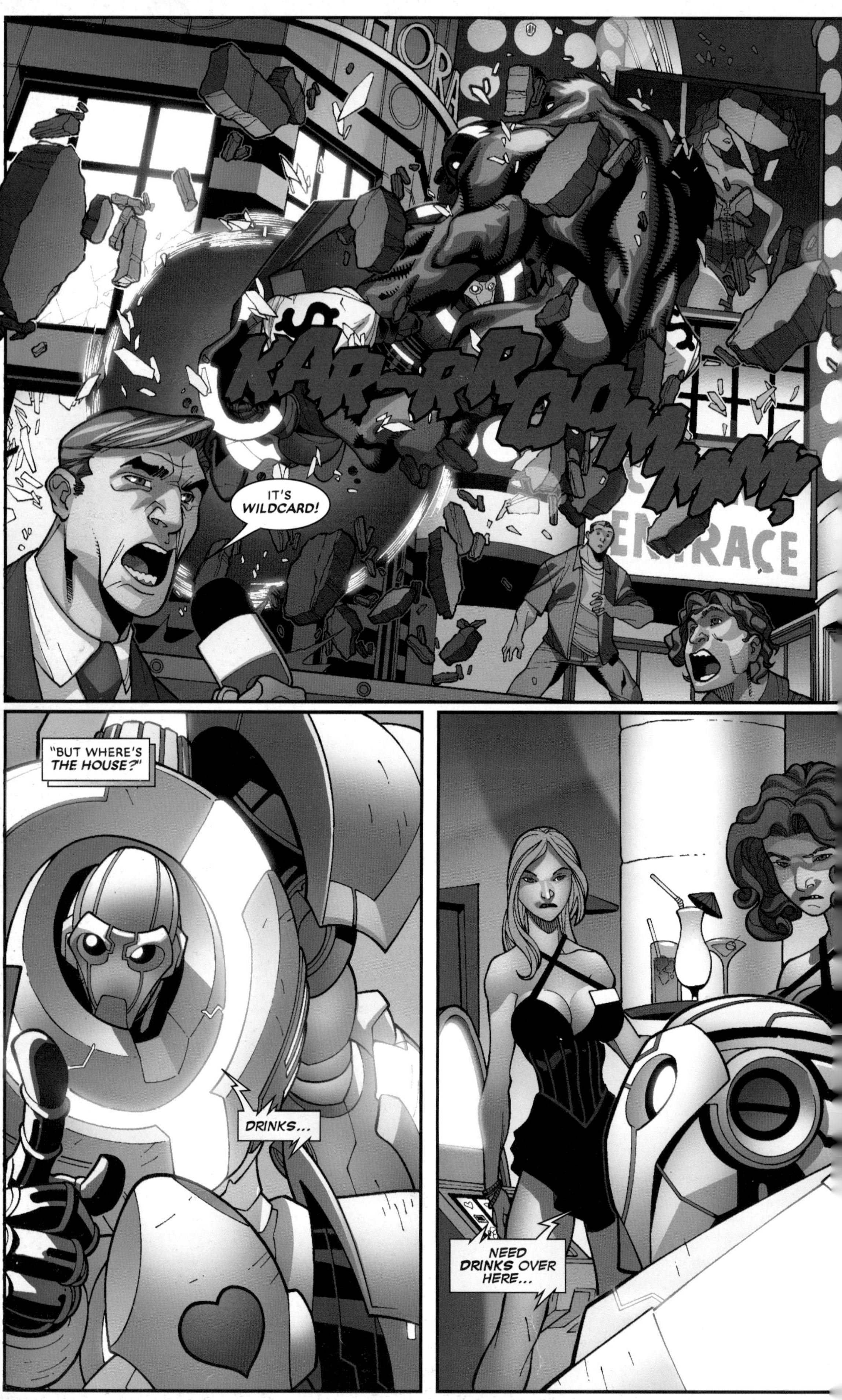
KAR-RROOMMMM!
IT'S WILDCARD!
"BUT WHERE'S THE HOUSE?"
DRINKS...
NEED DRINKS OVER HERE...

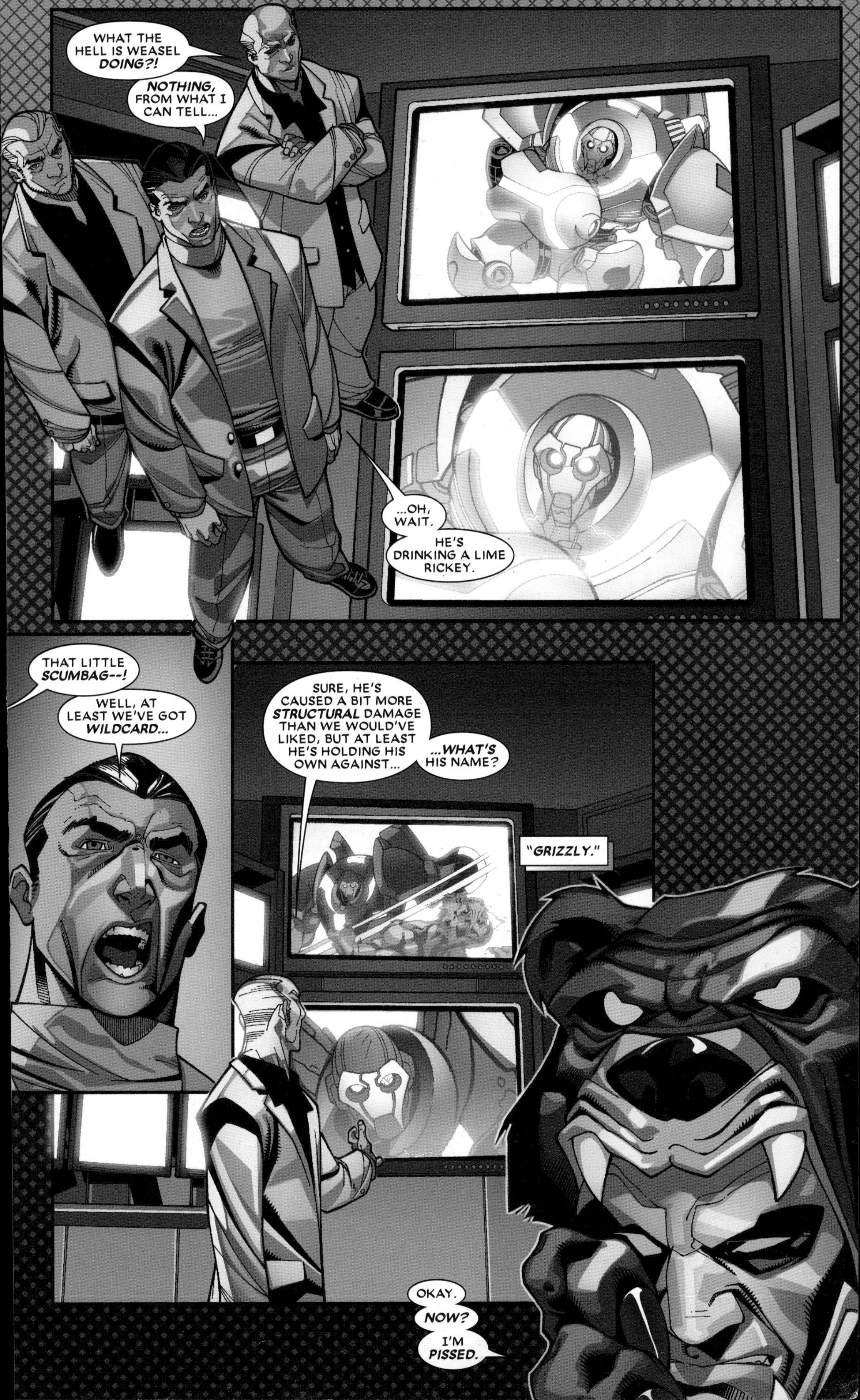
WHAT THE HELL IS WEASEL DOING?!
NOTHING, FROM WHAT I CAN TELL...
...OH, WAIT.
HE'S DRINKING A LIME RICKEY.
THAT LITTLE SCUMBAG--!
WELL, AT LEAST WE'VE GOT WILDCARD...
SURE, HE'S CAUSED A BIT MORE STRUCTURAL DAMAGE THAN WE WOULD'VE LIKED, BUT AT LEAST HE'S HOLDING HIS OWN AGAINST...
...WHAT'S HIS NAME?
"GRIZZLY."
OKAY.
NOW?
I'M PISSED.

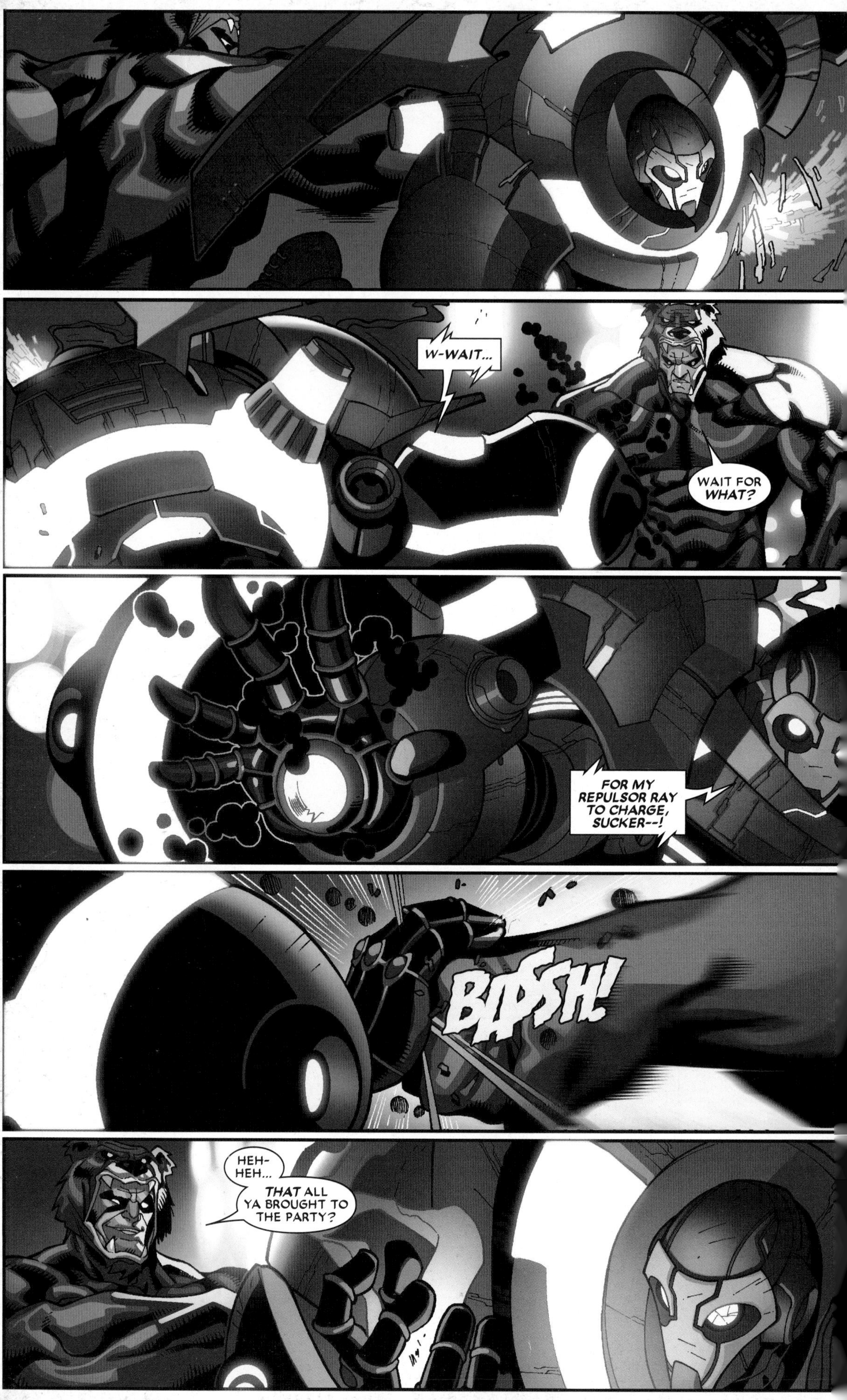
W-WAIT...
WAIT FOR *WHAT?*
FOR MY REPULSOR RAY TO CHARGE, SUCKER--!
BLASH!
HEH-HEH... *THAT* ALL YA BROUGHT TO THE PARTY?

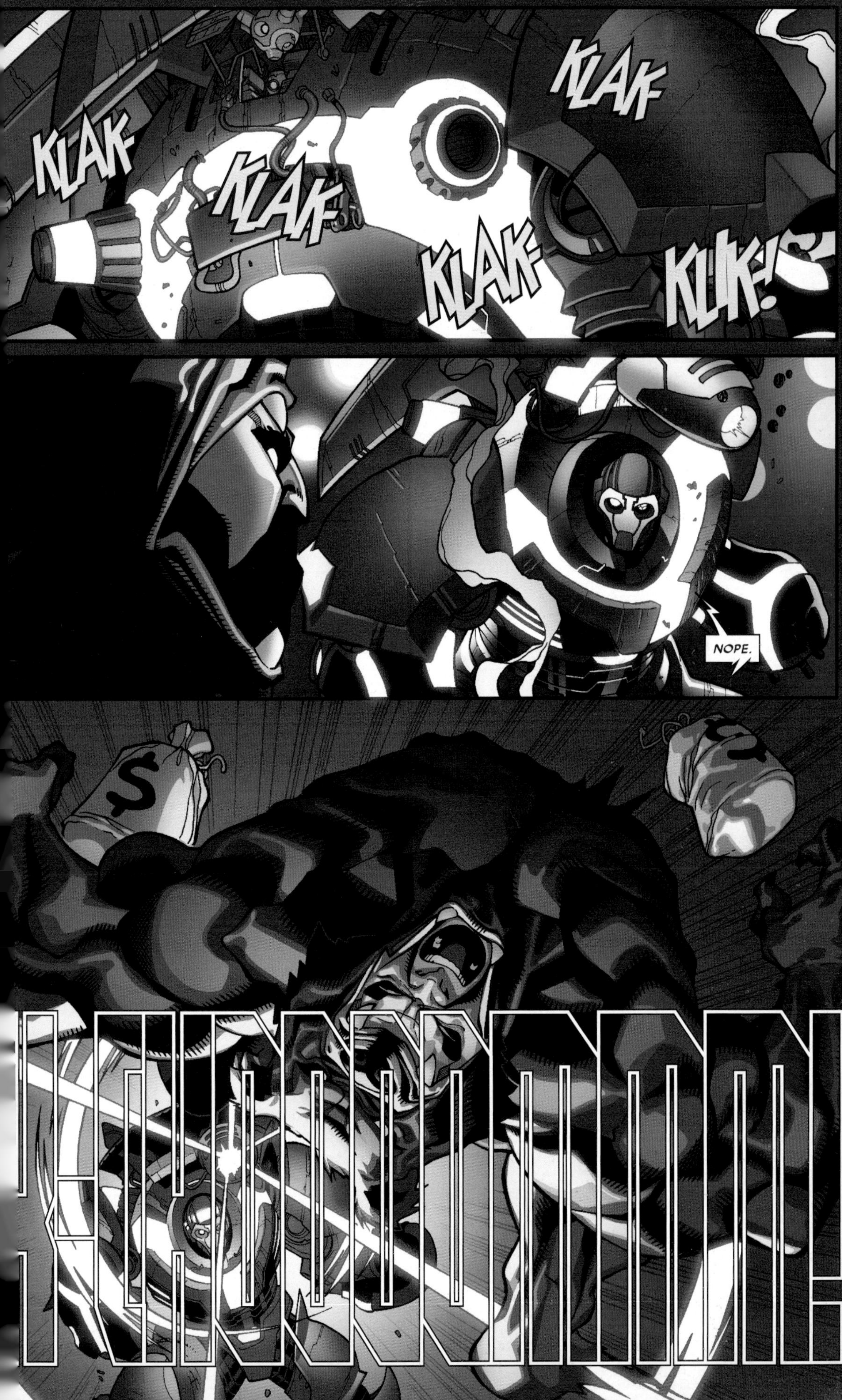
KLAK
KLAK
KLAK
KLAK
KLIK!
NOPE.

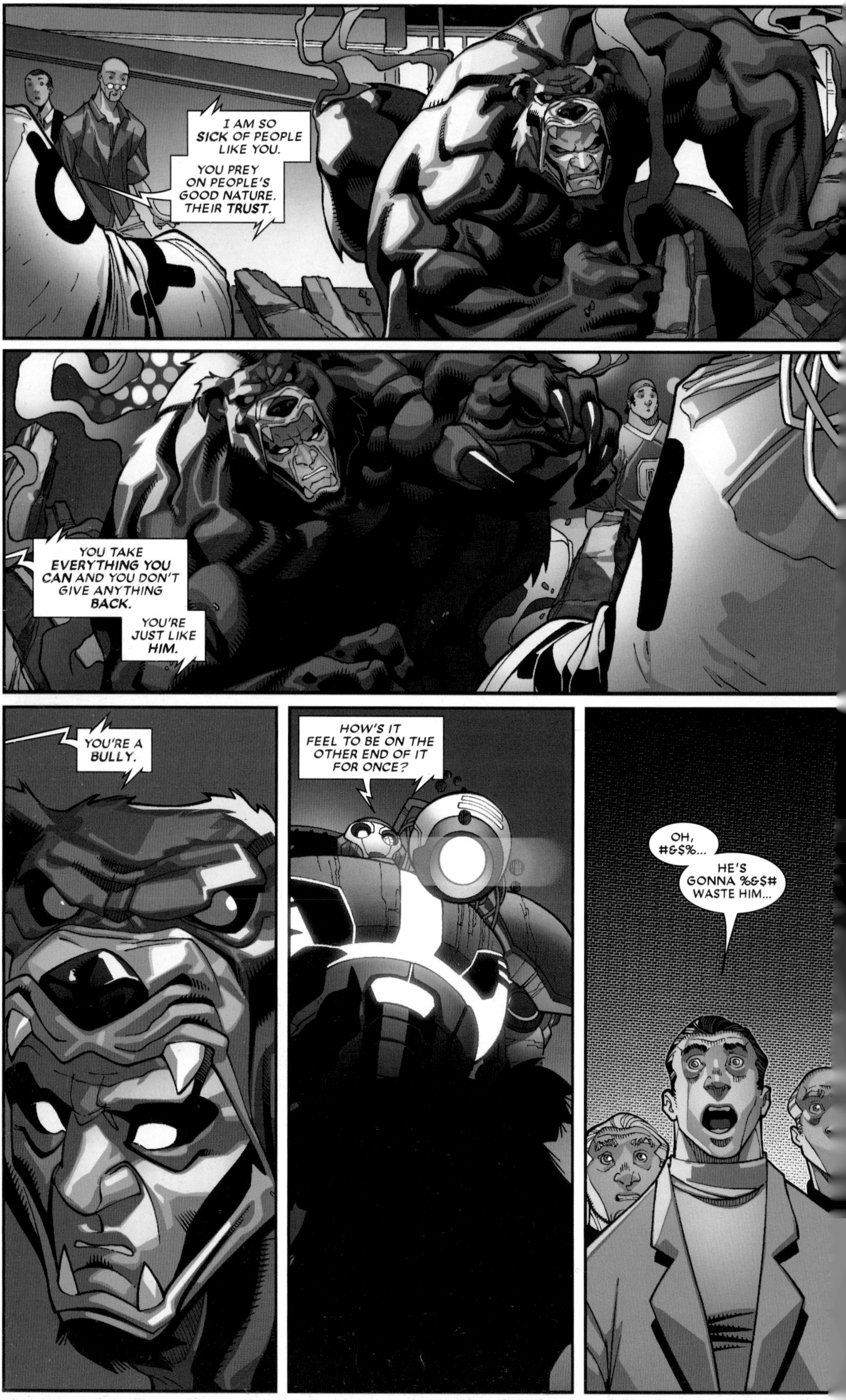
I AM SO SICK OF PEOPLE LIKE YOU.
YOU PREY ON PEOPLE'S GOOD NATURE. THEIR TRUST.
YOU TAKE EVERYTHING YOU CAN AND YOU DON'T GIVE ANYTHING BACK.
YOU'RE JUST LIKE HIM.
YOU'RE A BULLY.
HOW'S IT FEEL TO BE ON THE OTHER END OF IT FOR ONCE?
OH, #&$%...
HE'S GONNA %&$# WASTE HIM...

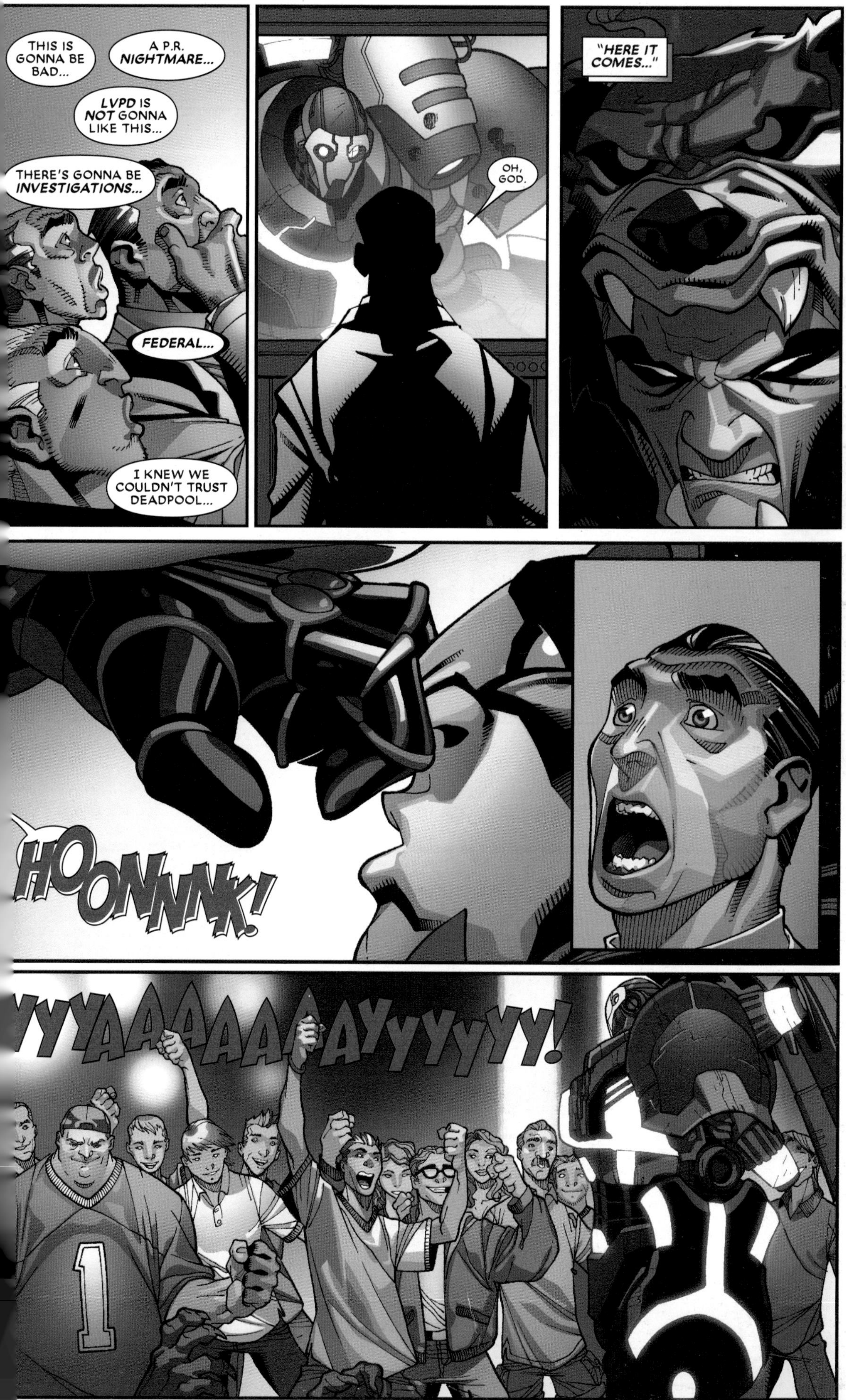
THIS IS GONNA BE BAD...
A P.R. NIGHTMARE...
LVPD IS NOT GONNA LIKE THIS...
THERE'S GONNA BE INVESTIGATIONS...
FEDERAL...
I KNEW WE COULDN'T TRUST DEADPOOL...
OH, GOD.
"HERE IT COMES..."
HOONNNK!
YYYAAAAAAAYYYYYYY!

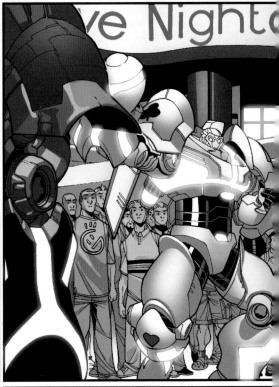

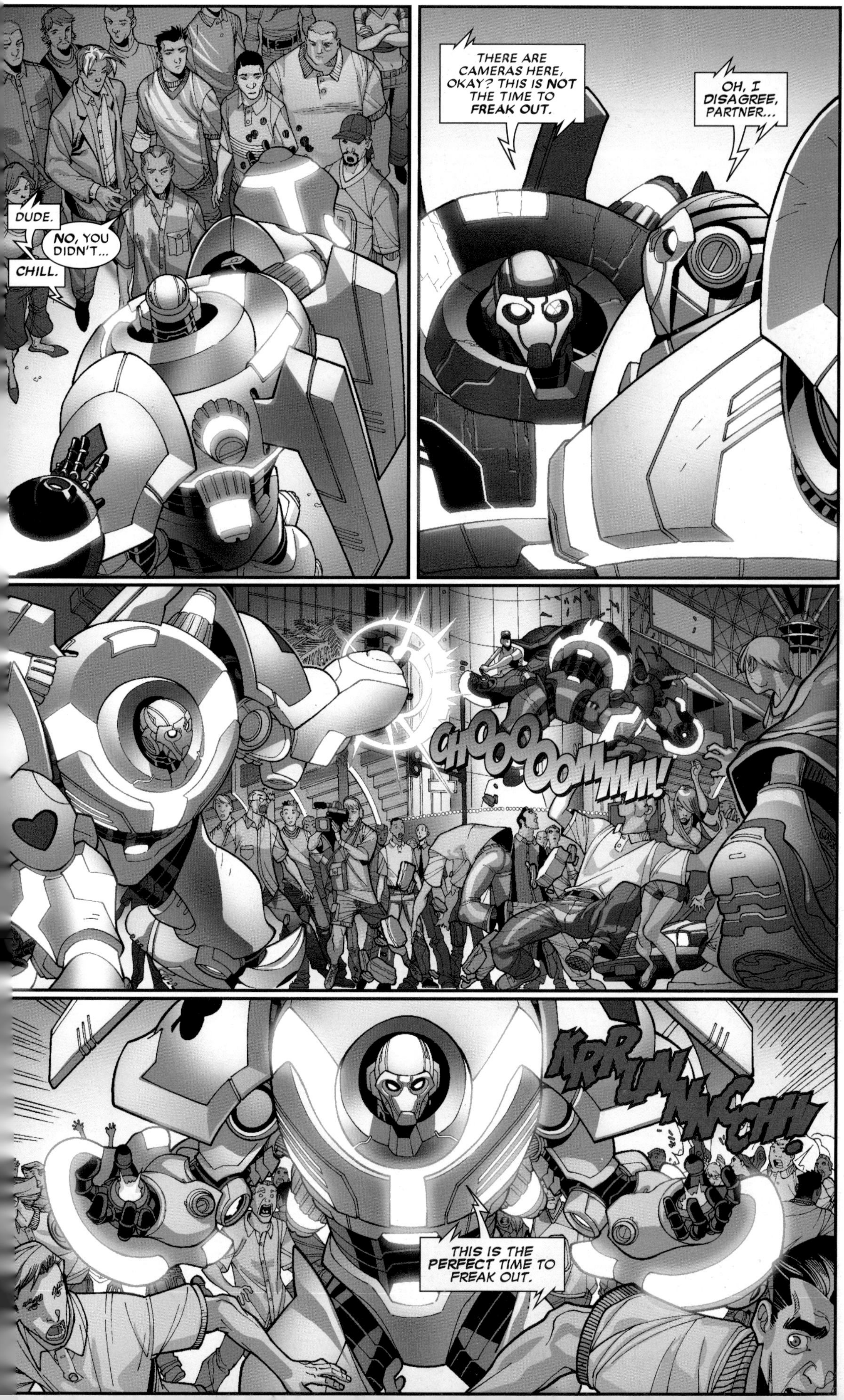
DUDE.
NO, YOU DIDN'T...
CHILL.
THERE ARE CAMERAS HERE, OKAY? THIS IS NOT THE TIME TO FREAK OUT.
OH, I DISAGREE, PARTNER...
CHOOOOOOMMMM!
KRRUNNNCHH
THIS IS THE PERFECT TIME TO FREAK OUT.

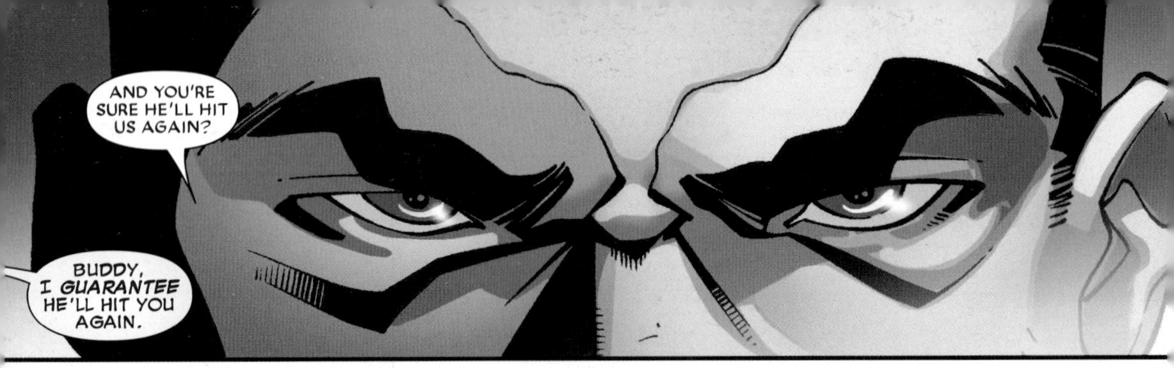
AND YOU'RE SURE HE'LL HIT US AGAIN?
BUDDY, I GUARANTEE HE'LL HIT YOU AGAIN.

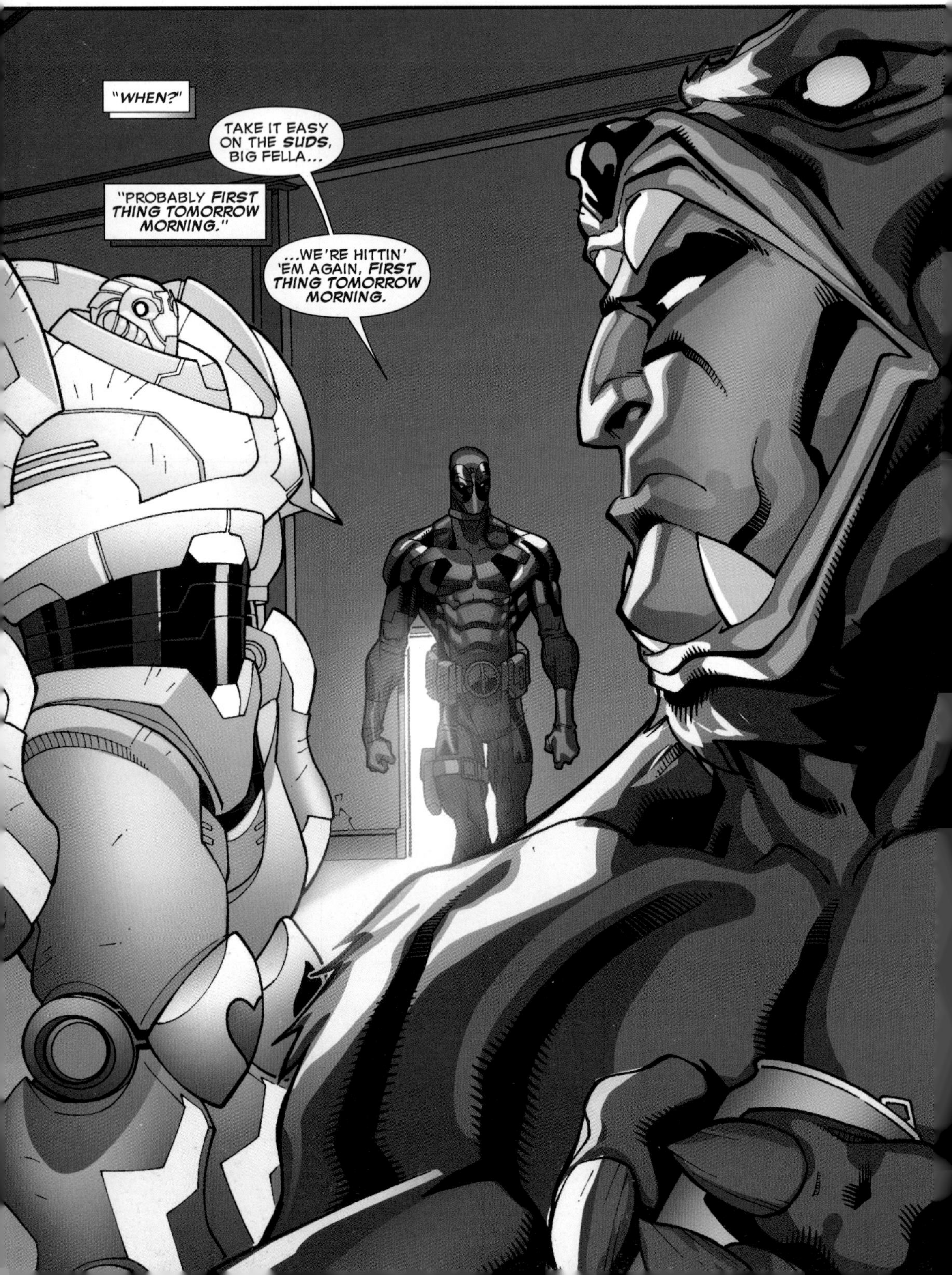
"WHEN?"
TAKE IT EASY ON THE SUDS, BIG FELLA...
"PROBABLY FIRST THING TOMORROW MORNING."
...WE'RE HITTIN' 'EM AGAIN, FIRST THING TOMORROW MORNING.

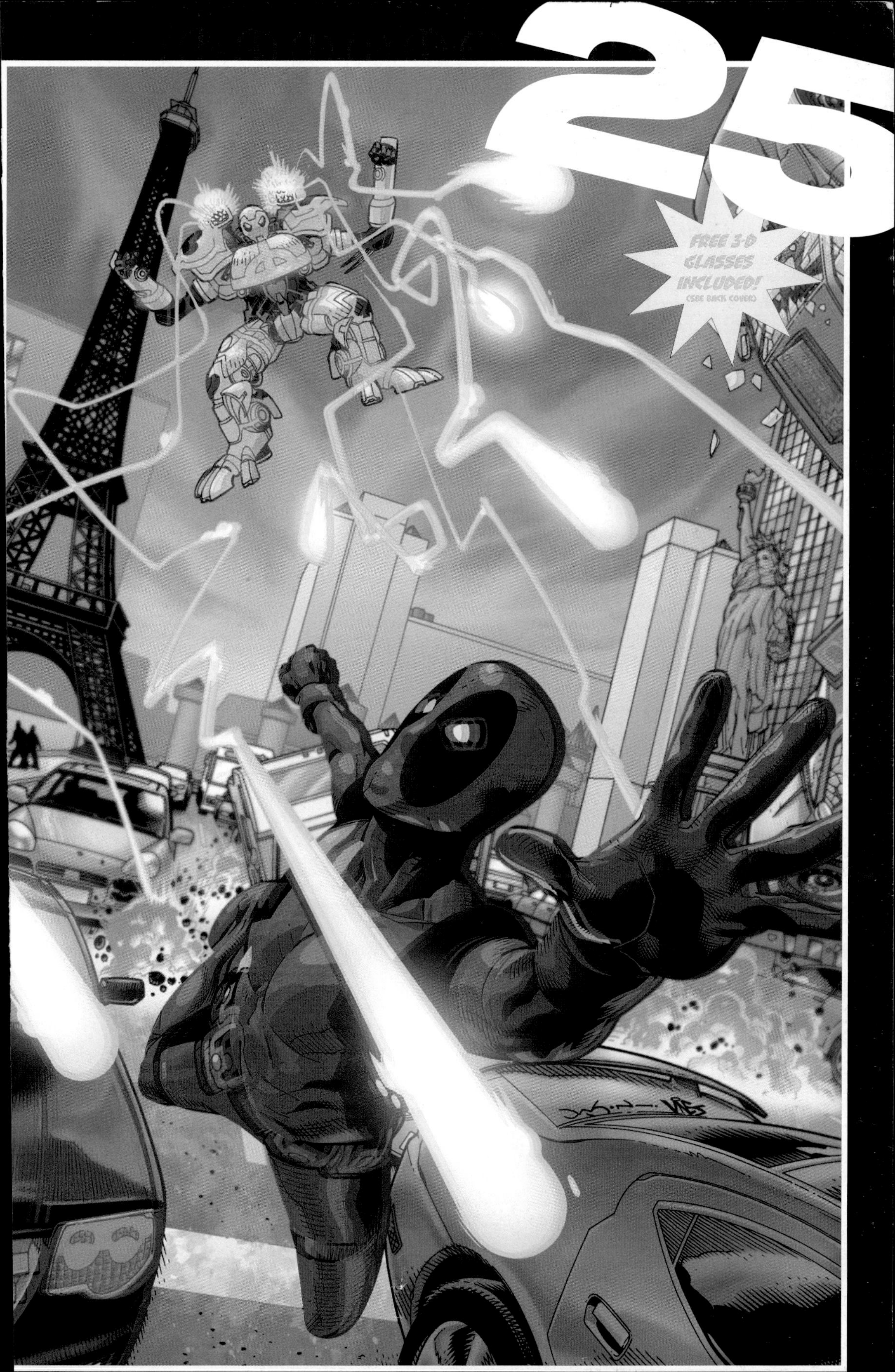
25
FREE 3-D GLASSES INCLUDED!
(SEE BACK COVER)

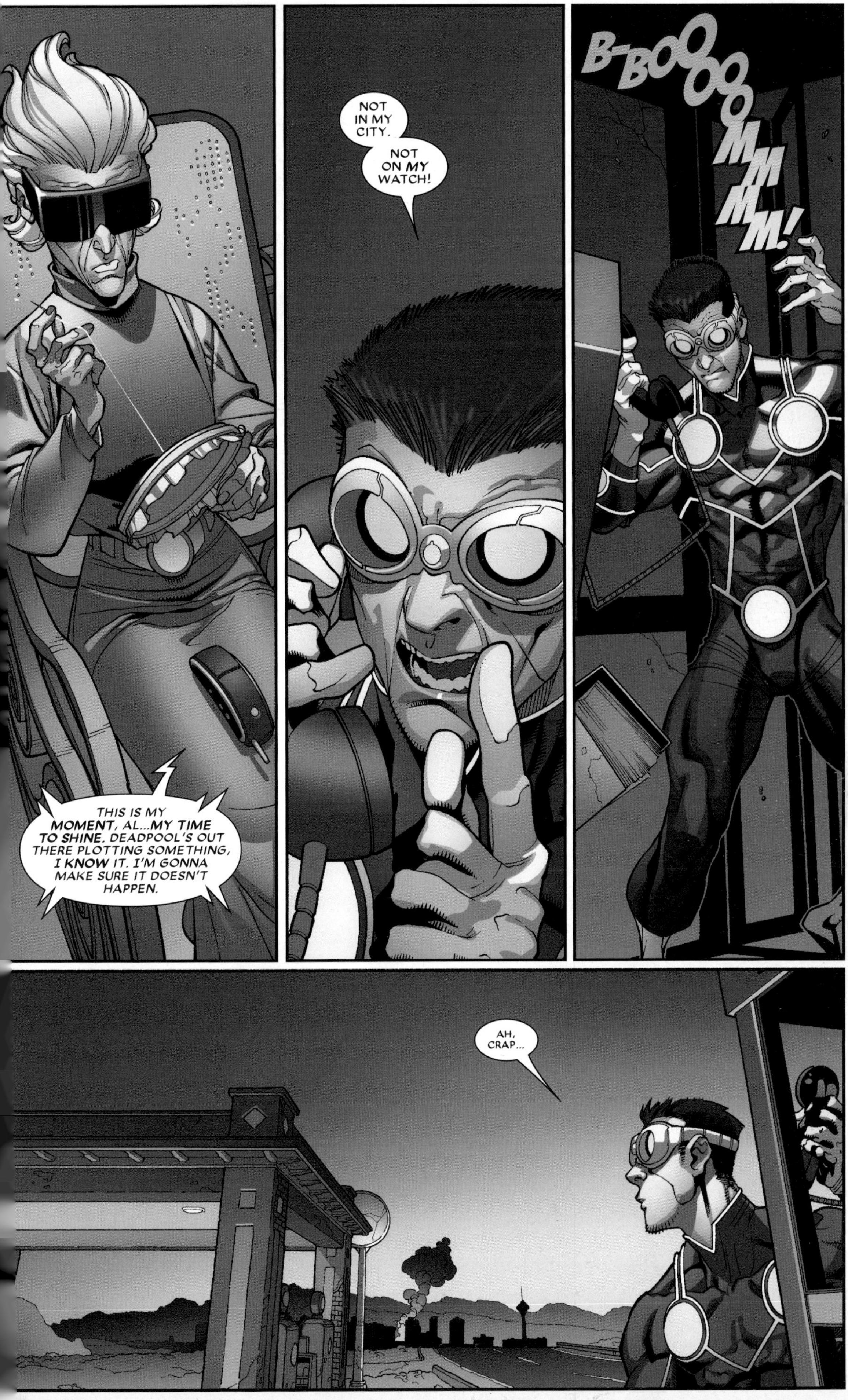
THIS IS MY MOMENT, AL...MY TIME TO SHINE. DEADPOOL'S OUT THERE PLOTTING SOMETHING, I KNOW IT. I'M GONNA MAKE SURE IT DOESN'T HAPPEN.
NOT IN MY CITY.
NOT ON MY WATCH!
B-BOOOOOOMMMMM!
AH, CRAP...

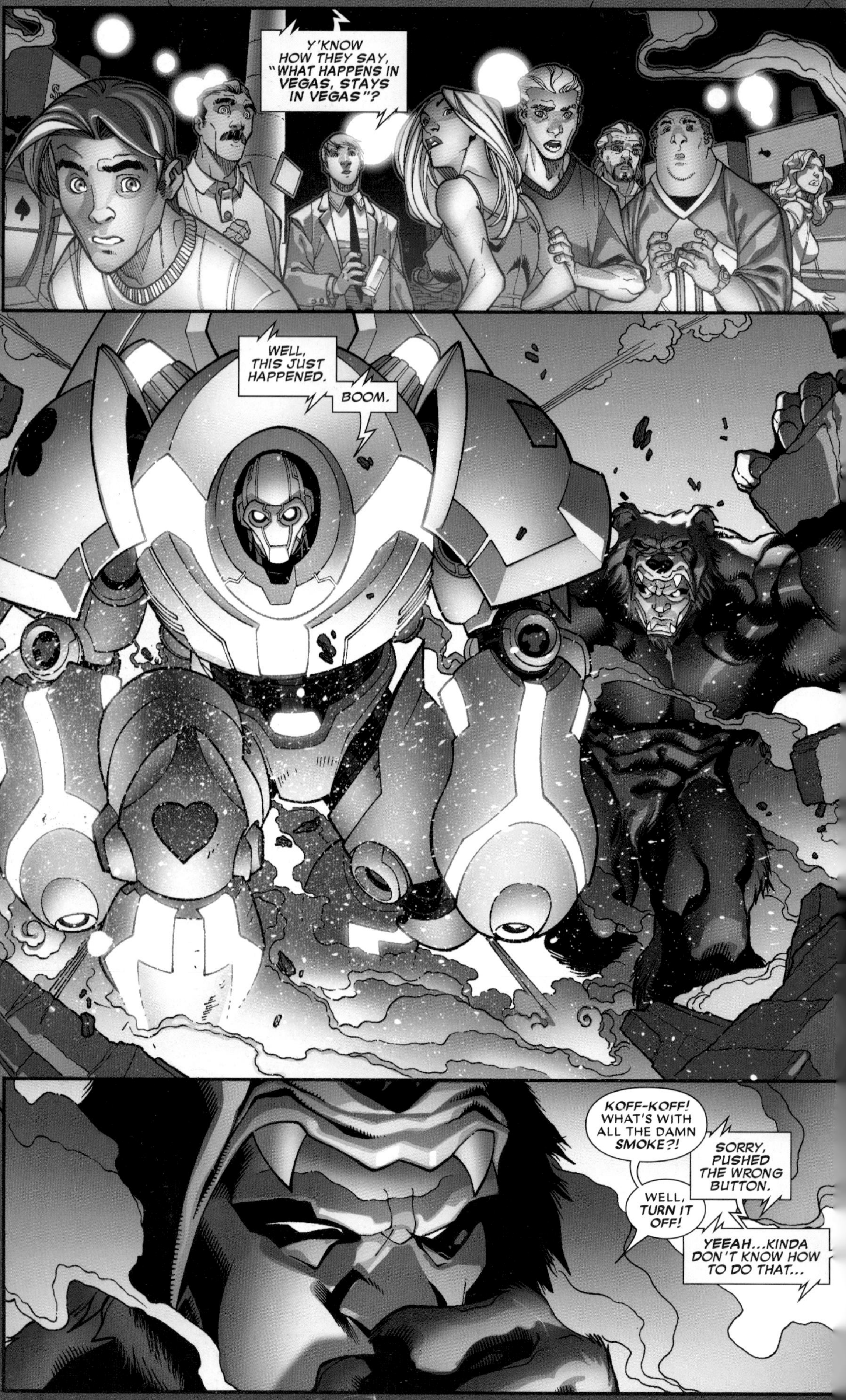
Y'KNOW HOW THEY SAY, "WHAT HAPPENS IN VEGAS, STAYS IN VEGAS"?
WELL, THIS JUST HAPPENED.
BOOM.
KOFF-KOFF! WHAT'S WITH ALL THE DAMN SMOKE?!
SORRY, PUSHED THE WRONG BUTTON.
WELL, TURN IT OFF!
YEEAH...KINDA DON'T KNOW HOW TO DO THAT...

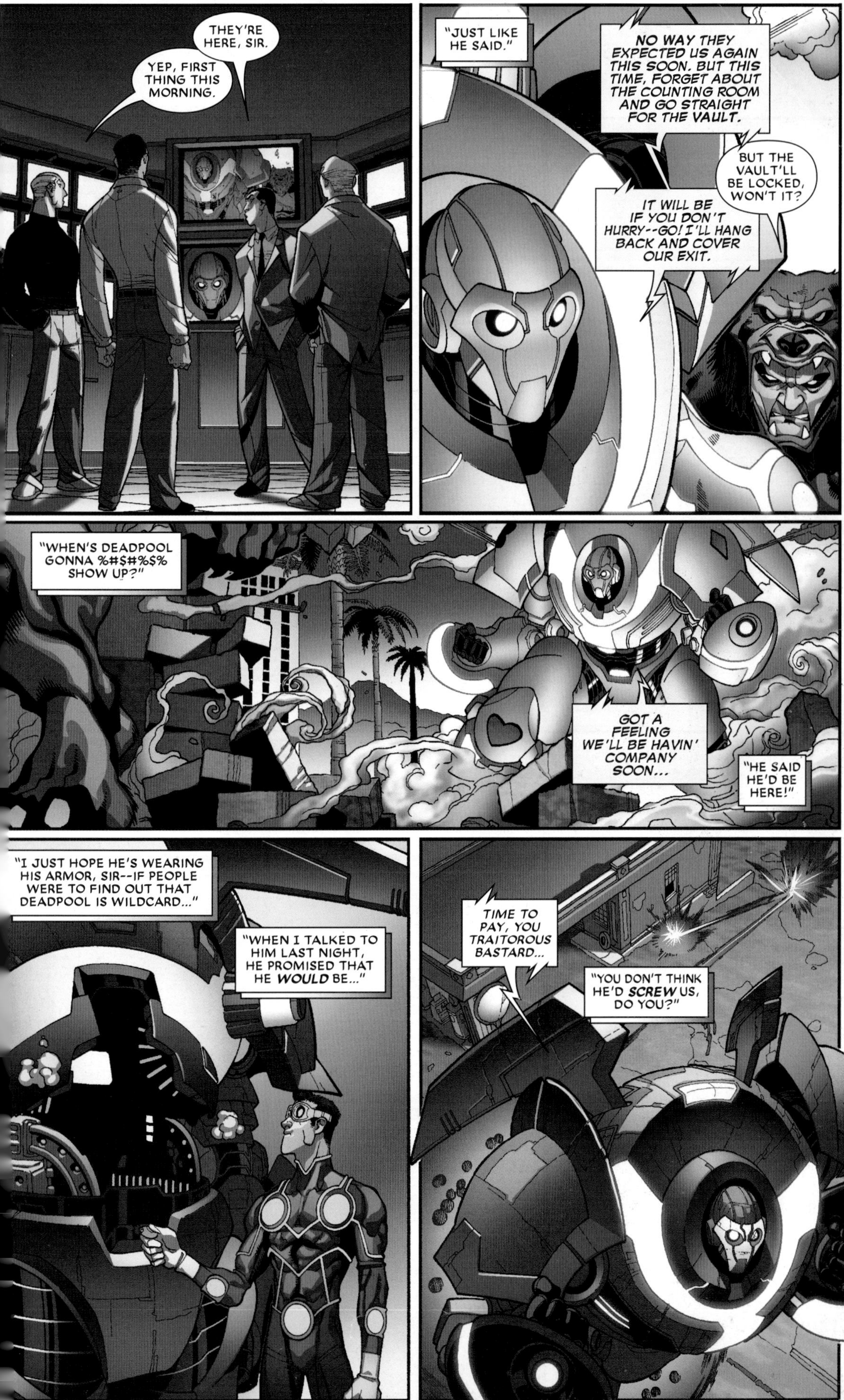
THEY'RE HERE, SIR.
YEP, FIRST THING THIS MORNING.
"JUST LIKE HE SAID."
NO WAY THEY EXPECTED US AGAIN THIS SOON. BUT THIS TIME, FORGET ABOUT THE COUNTING ROOM AND GO STRAIGHT FOR THE VAULT.
BUT THE VAULT'LL BE LOCKED, WON'T IT?
IT WILL BE IF YOU DON'T HURRY--GO! I'LL HANG BACK AND COVER OUR EXIT.
"WHEN'S DEADPOOL GONNA %#$#%$% SHOW UP?"
GOT A FEELING WE'LL BE HAVIN' COMPANY SOON...
"HE SAID HE'D BE HERE!"
"I JUST HOPE HE'S WEARING HIS ARMOR, SIR--IF PEOPLE WERE TO FIND OUT THAT DEADPOOL IS WILDCARD..."
"WHEN I TALKED TO HIM LAST NIGHT, HE PROMISED THAT HE WOULD BE..."
TIME TO PAY, YOU TRAITOROUS BASTARD...
"YOU DON'T THINK HE'D SCREW US, DO YOU?"

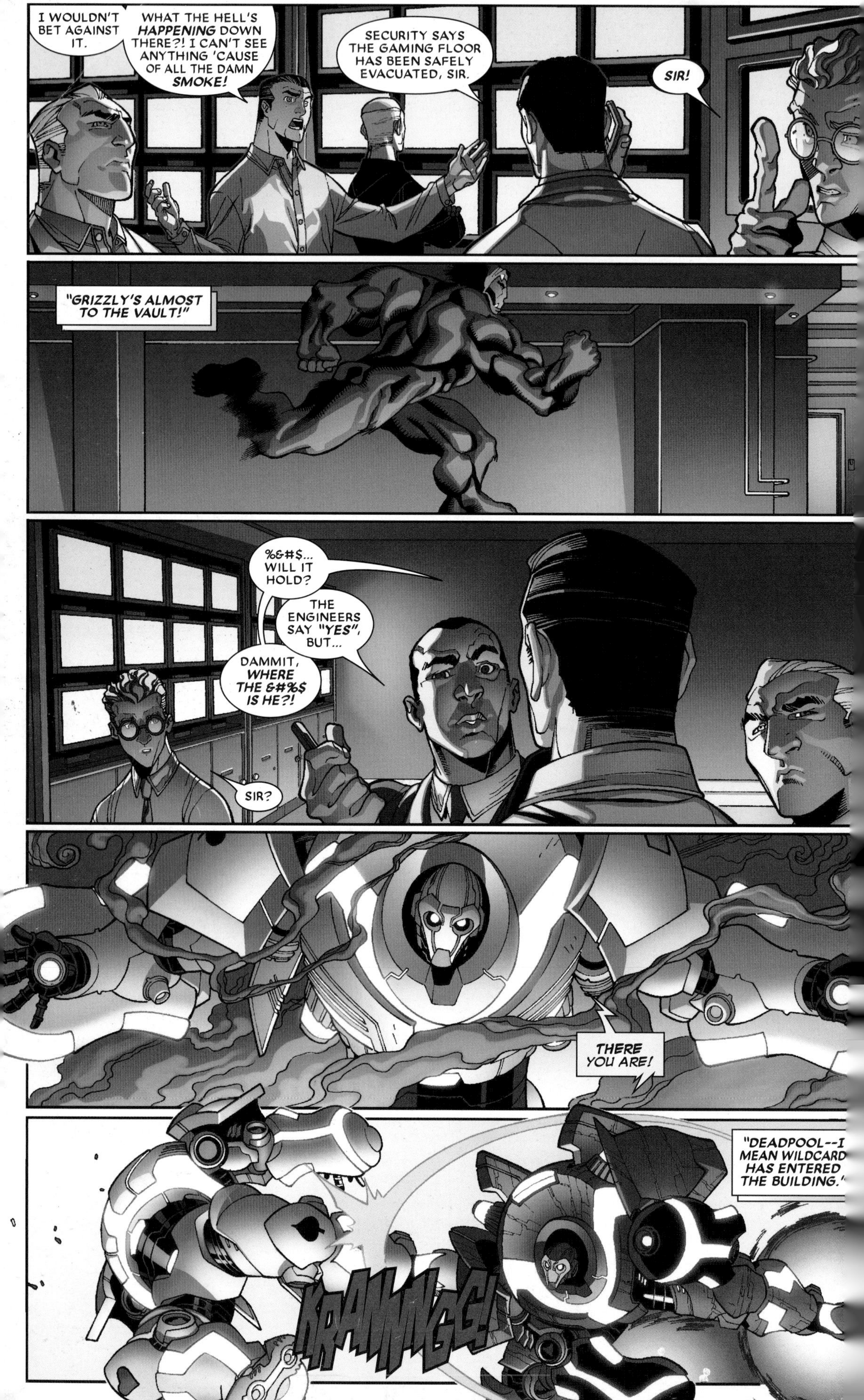
I WOULDN'T BET AGAINST IT.
WHAT THE HELL'S HAPPENING DOWN THERE?! I CAN'T SEE ANYTHING 'CAUSE OF ALL THE DAMN SMOKE!
SECURITY SAYS THE GAMING FLOOR HAS BEEN SAFELY EVACUATED, SIR.
SIR!
"GRIZZLY'S ALMOST TO THE VAULT!"
%&#$... WILL IT HOLD?
THE ENGINEERS SAY "YES", BUT...
DAMMIT, WHERE THE &#%$ IS HE?!
SIR?
THERE YOU ARE!
"DEADPOOL--I MEAN WILDCARD HAS ENTERED THE BUILDING."
KRANNGG!

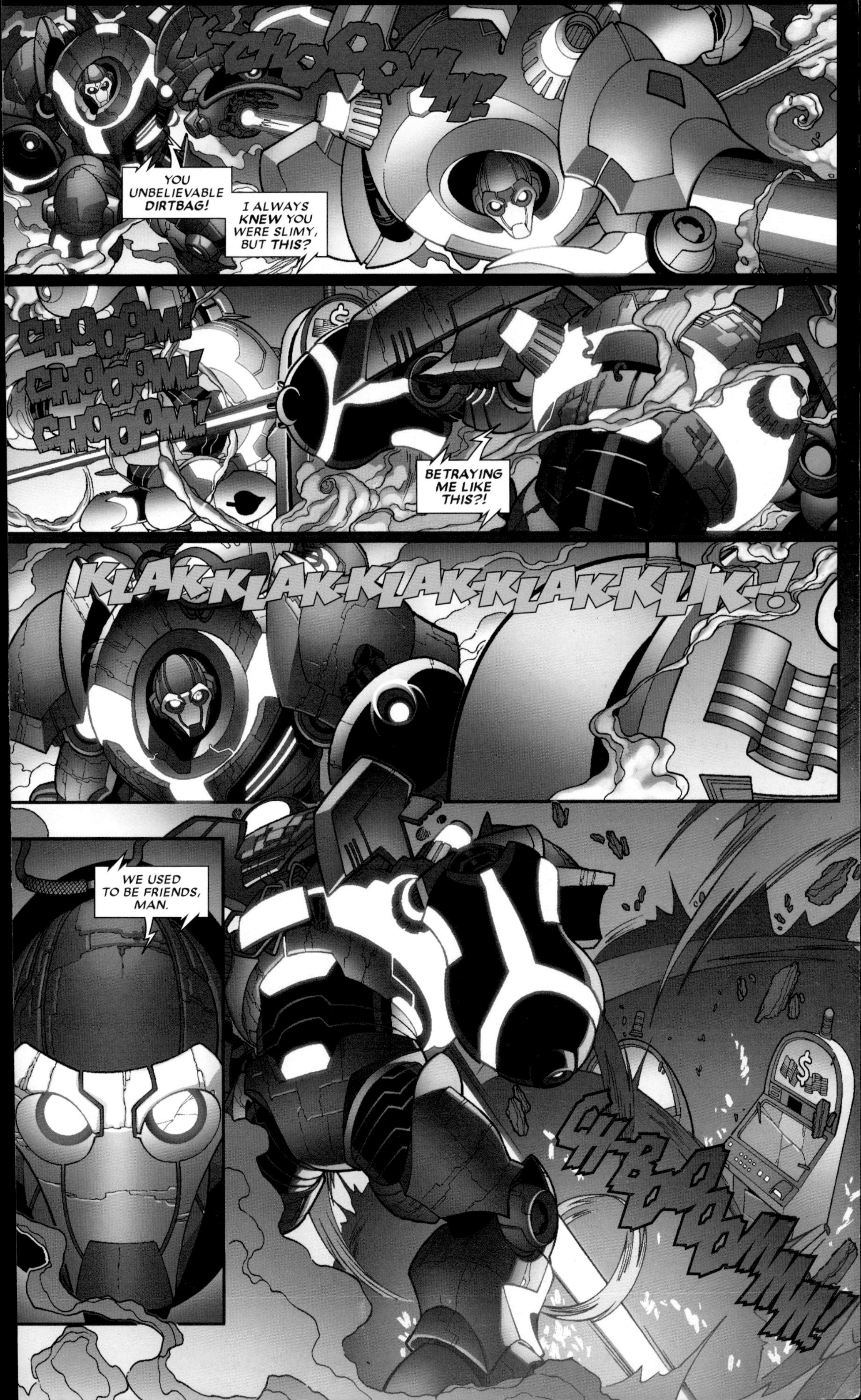
K-CHOOOOM!
YOU UNBELIEVABLE DIRTBAG!
I ALWAYS KNEW YOU WERE SLIMY, BUT THIS?
CHOOOM! CHOOOM! CHOOOM!
BETRAYING ME LIKE THIS?!
KLAK-KLAK-KLAK-KLAK-KLIK-!
WE USED TO BE FRIENDS, MAN.
CHBOOOMM!

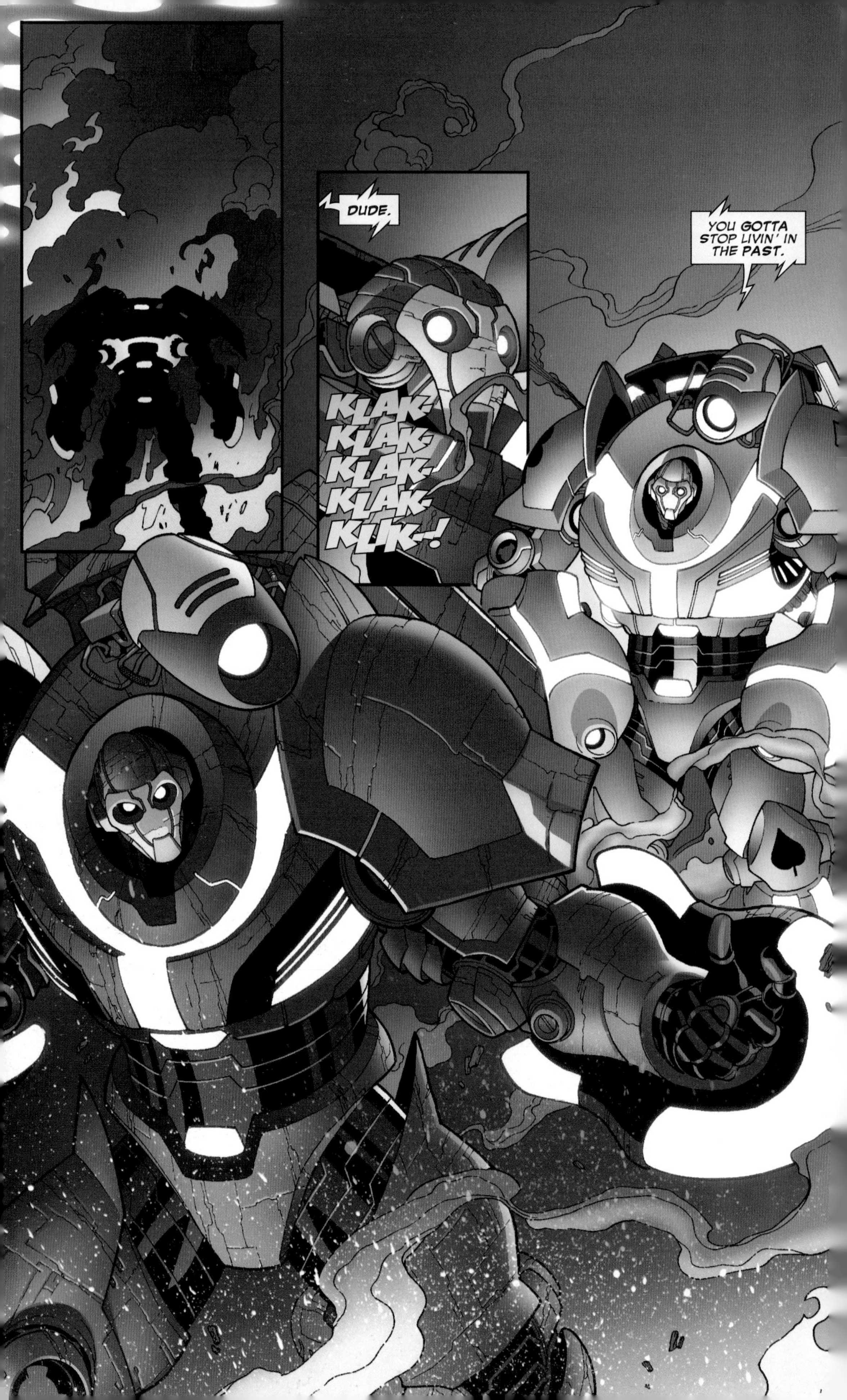
DUDE.
KLAK-KLAK-KLAK-KLAK-KLIK-!
YOU GOTTA STOP LIVIN' IN THE PAST.

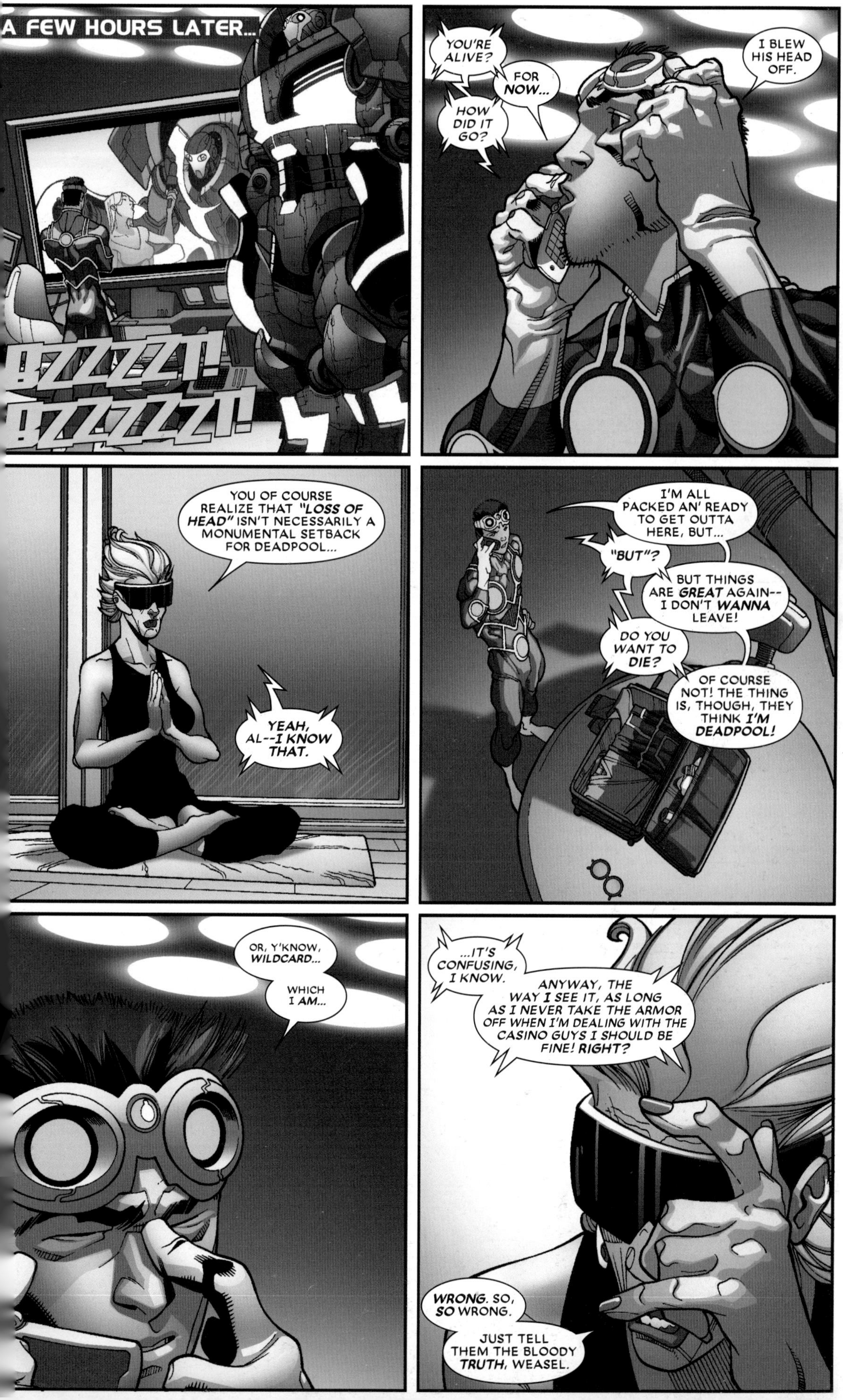
A FEW HOURS LATER...
BZZZZZT! BZZZZZT!
YOU'RE ALIVE?
HOW DID IT GO?
FOR NOW...
I BLEW HIS HEAD OFF.
YOU OF COURSE REALIZE THAT "LOSS OF HEAD" ISN'T NECESSARILY A MONUMENTAL SETBACK FOR DEADPOOL...
YEAH, AL--I KNOW THAT.
I'M ALL PACKED AN' READY TO GET OUTTA HERE, BUT...
"BUT"?
BUT THINGS ARE GREAT AGAIN--I DON'T WANNA LEAVE!
DO YOU WANT TO DIE?
OF COURSE NOT! THE THING IS, THOUGH, THEY THINK I'M DEADPOOL!
OR, Y'KNOW, WILDCARD...
WHICH I AM...
...IT'S CONFUSING, I KNOW.
ANYWAY, THE WAY I SEE IT, AS LONG AS I NEVER TAKE THE ARMOR OFF WHEN I'M DEALING WITH THE CASINO GUYS I SHOULD BE FINE! RIGHT?
WRONG. SO, SO WRONG.
JUST TELL THEM THE BLOODY TRUTH, WEASEL.

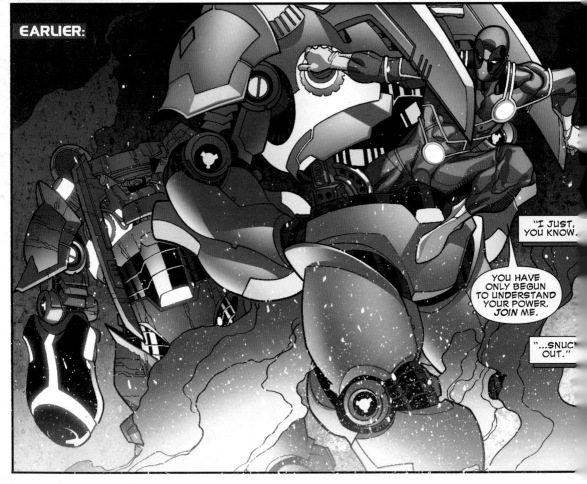

EARLIER:

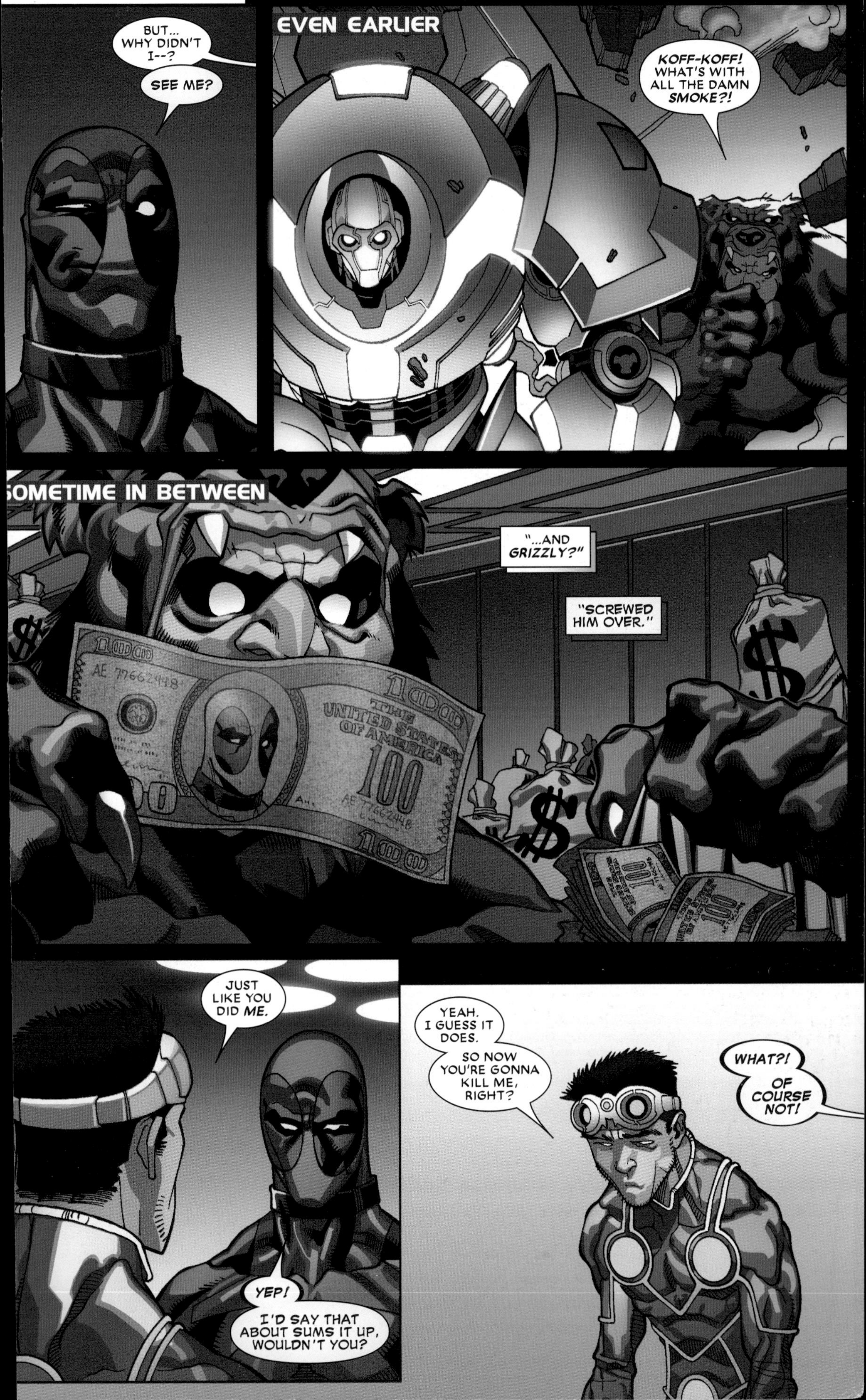
BUT... WHY DIDN'T I--?
SEE ME?
EVEN EARLIER
KOFF-KOFF! WHAT'S WITH ALL THE DAMN SMOKE?!
SOMETIME IN BETWEEN
"...AND GRIZZLY?"
"SCREWED HIM OVER."
JUST LIKE YOU DID ME.
YEP!
I'D SAY THAT ABOUT SUMS IT UP, WOULDN'T YOU?
YEAH. I GUESS IT DOES.
SO NOW YOU'RE GONNA KILL ME, RIGHT?
WHAT?!
OF COURSE NOT!

I'M A HERO, DUDE--HEROES DON'T GO AROUND KILLING PEOPLE, WILLY-NILLY!

SO...NOW YOU'RE GONNA KILL ME?

OH, FOR...

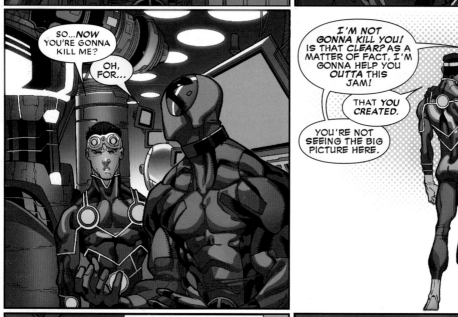

I'M NOT GONNA KILL YOU! IS THAT CLEAR? AS A MATTER OF FACT, I'M GONNA HELP YOU OUTTA THIS JAM!

THAT YOU CREATED.

YOU'RE NOT SEEING THE BIG PICTURE HERE.

YOU WERE A CRAPPY HERO, DUDE. LET'S FACE IT-- SOONER OR LATER, YOU WERE GONNA BLOW IT.

BUT NOW, WITH ME TAKING OVER--

WAIT, YOU'RE TAKING OVER? TAKING OVER WHAT?

THAT. DUH.

BUT... WHAT ABOUT ME?

YOU'RE GONNA HAFTA DISAPPEAR.

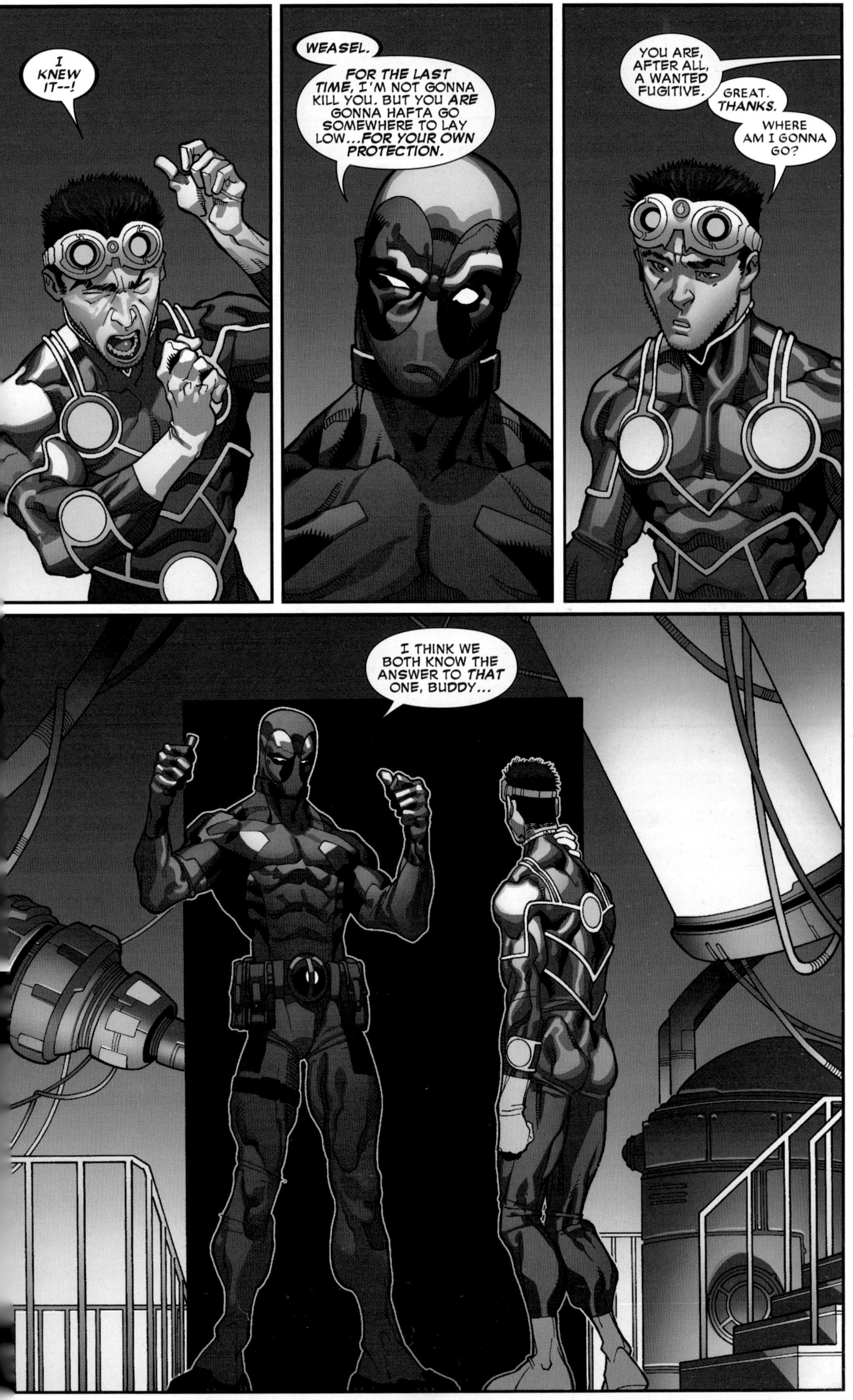
I KNEW IT--!
WEASEL.
FOR THE LAST TIME, I'M NOT GONNA KILL YOU. BUT YOU ARE GONNA HAFTA GO SOMEWHERE TO LAY LOW...FOR YOUR OWN PROTECTION.
YOU ARE, AFTER ALL, A WANTED FUGITIVE.
GREAT. THANKS.
WHERE AM I GONNA GO?
I THINK WE BOTH KNOW THE ANSWER TO THAT ONE, BUDDY...

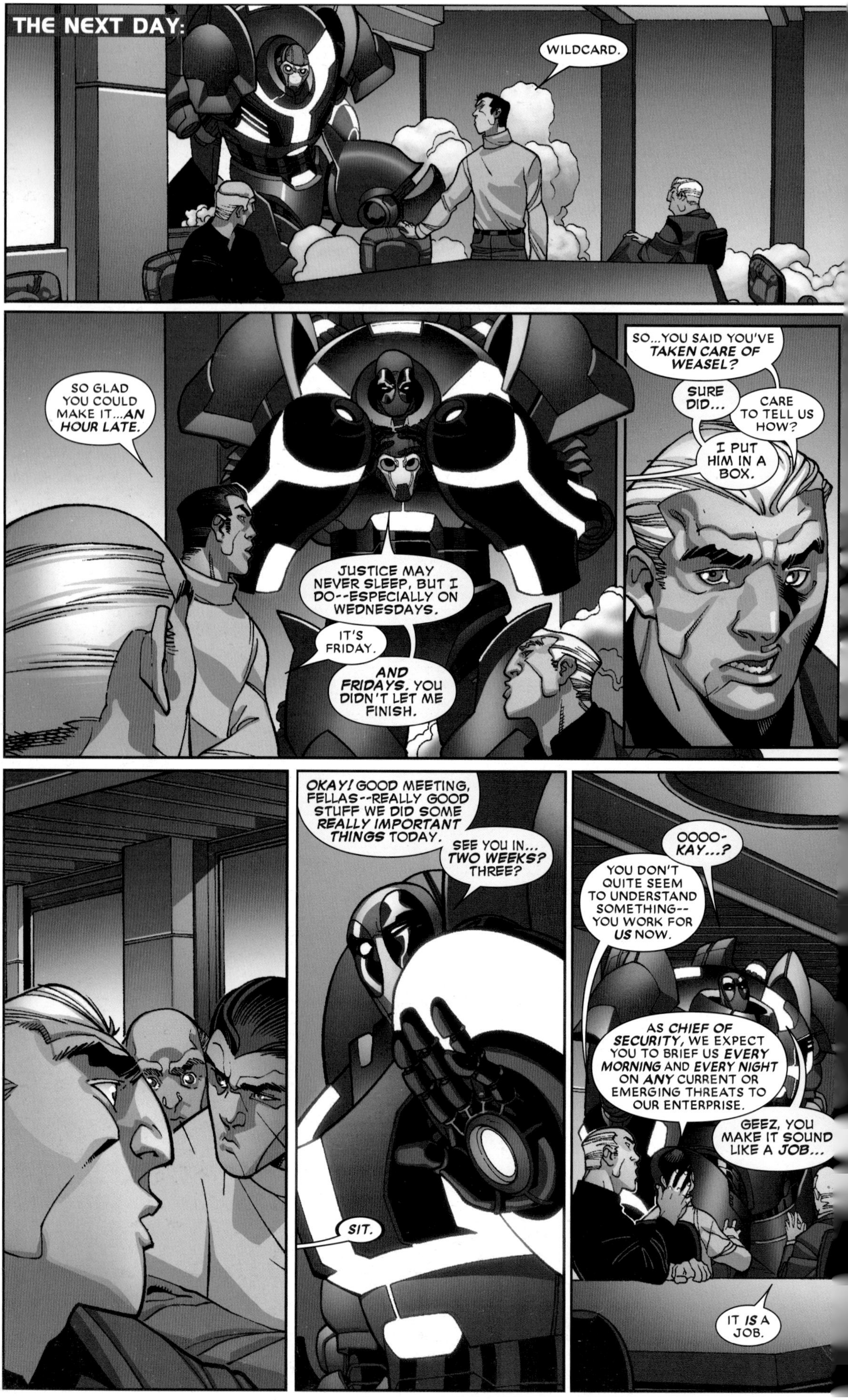
THE NEXT DAY:
WILDCARD.
SO GLAD YOU COULD MAKE IT...AN HOUR LATE.
JUSTICE MAY NEVER SLEEP, BUT I DO--ESPECIALLY ON WEDNESDAYS.
IT'S FRIDAY.
AND FRIDAYS. YOU DIDN'T LET ME FINISH.
SO...YOU SAID YOU'VE TAKEN CARE OF WEASEL?
SURE DID...
CARE TO TELL US HOW?
I PUT HIM IN A BOX.
OKAY! GOOD MEETING, FELLAS--REALLY GOOD STUFF WE DID SOME REALLY IMPORTANT THINGS TODAY.
SEE YOU IN... TWO WEEKS? THREE?
SIT.
OOOO-KAY...?
YOU DON'T QUITE SEEM TO UNDERSTAND SOMETHING--YOU WORK FOR US NOW.
AS CHIEF OF SECURITY, WE EXPECT YOU TO BRIEF US EVERY MORNING AND EVERY NIGHT ON ANY CURRENT OR EMERGING THREATS TO OUR ENTERPRISE.
GEEZ, YOU MAKE IT SOUND LIKE A JOB...
IT IS A JOB.

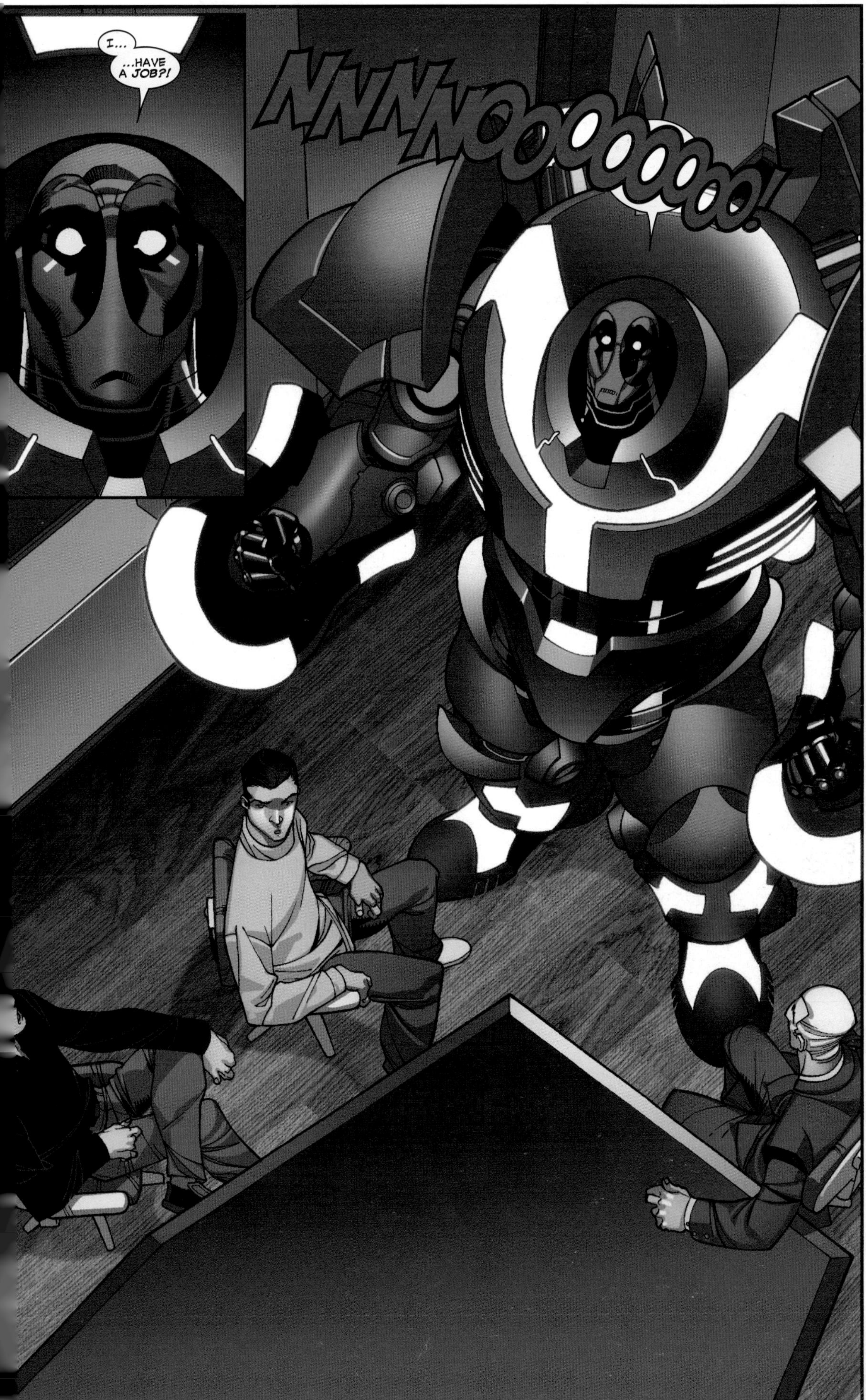
I...
...HAVE A JOB?!
NNNNOOOOOOOOO!

26

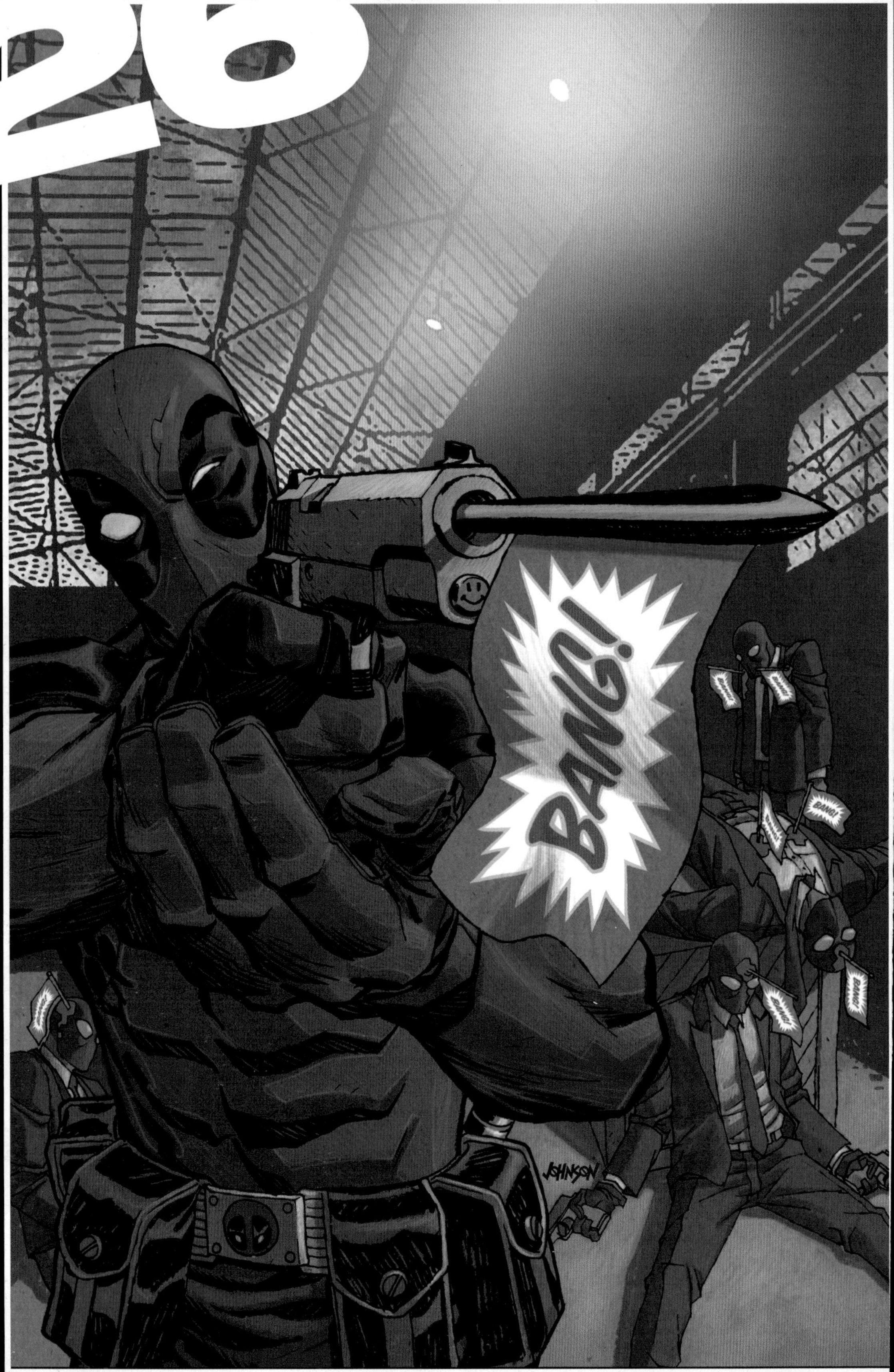
BANG!
JOHNSON

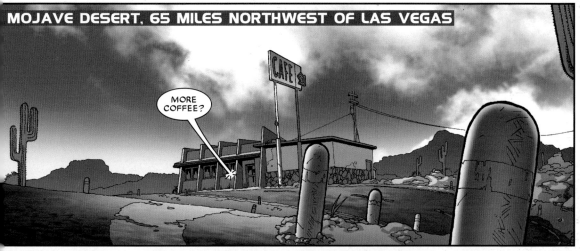

MORE COFFEE?

NAH, I'M GOOD. THIS COVER IT?

UHH...*YEAH*, THAT'S *MORE* THAN--

JUST KEEP IT.

WHEW!

THAT *YOUR* BIKE OUT FRONT?

YEAH.

WELL, BE CAREFUL--IT'S *ALREADY* OVER A HUNDRED DEGREES OUT THERE, AN' THE WEATHER MAN SAYS IT'S JUST GONNA GET HOTTER.

THE WEATHER MAN'S RIGHT.

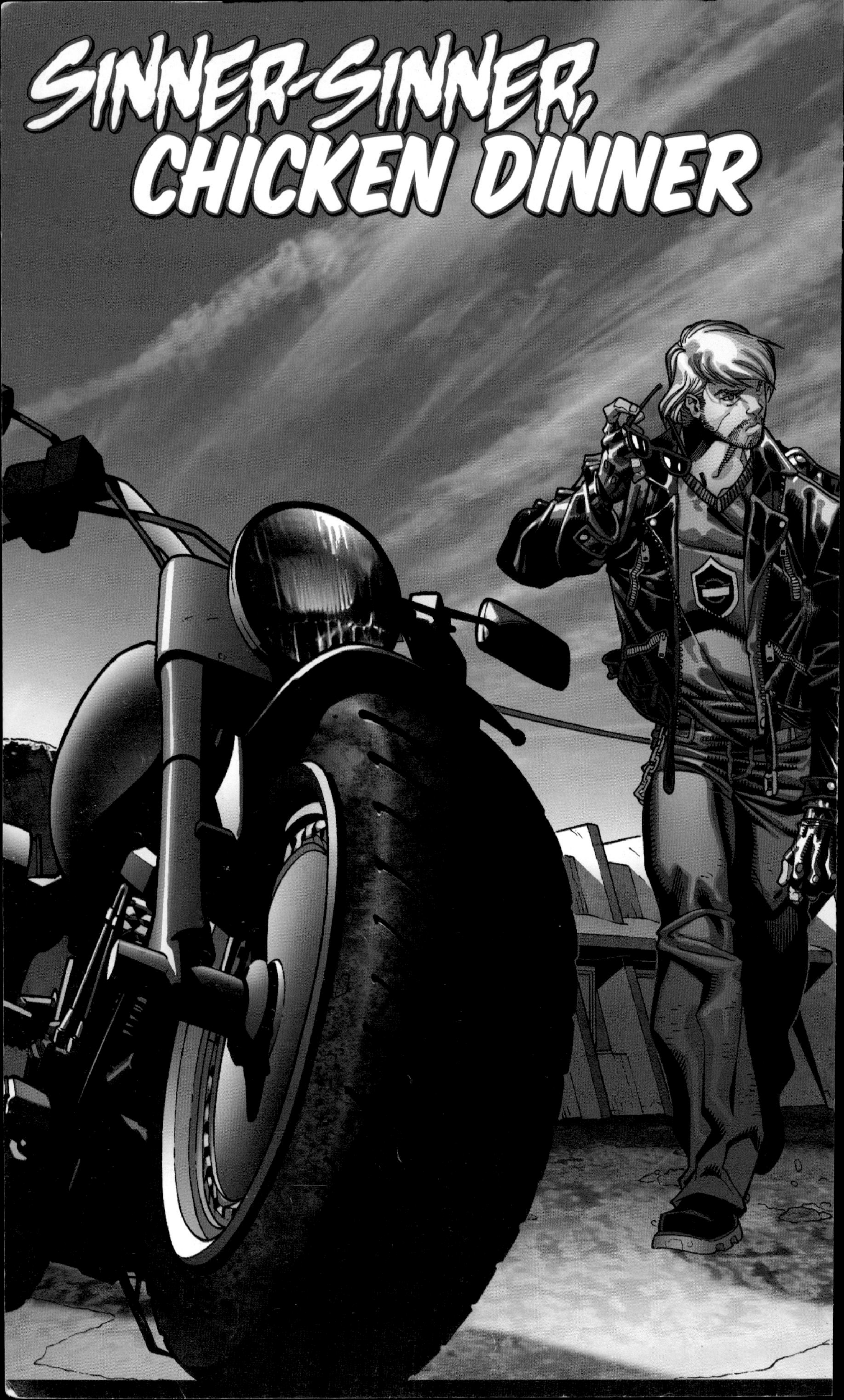
SINNER-SINNER, CHICKEN DINNER

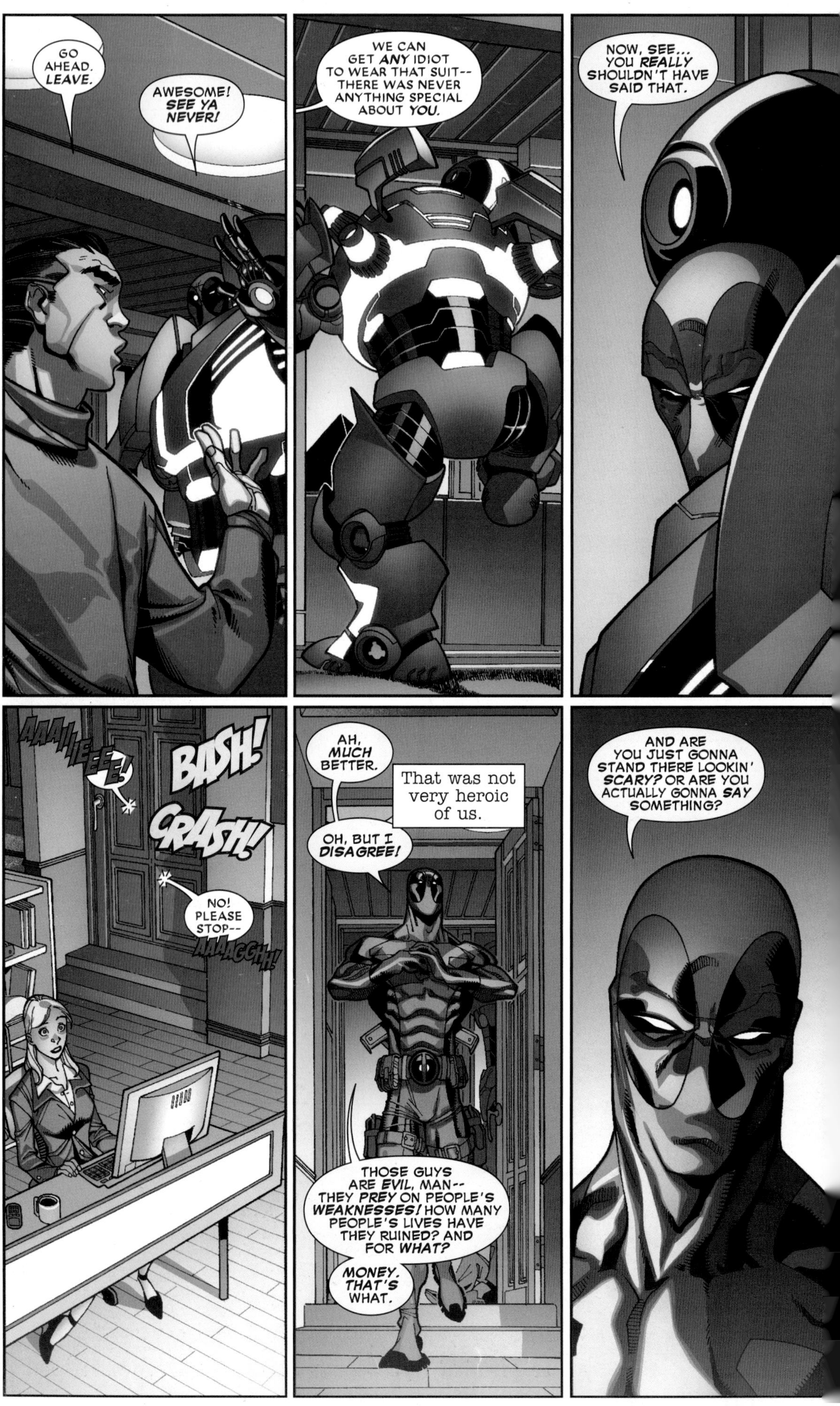

GO AHEAD. LEAVE.
AWESOME! SEE YA NEVER!
WE CAN GET ANY IDIOT TO WEAR THAT SUIT-- THERE WAS NEVER ANYTHING SPECIAL ABOUT YOU.
NOW, SEE... YOU REALLY SHOULDN'T HAVE SAID THAT.
AAAIIIEEEE!
BASH!
CRASH!
NO! PLEASE STOP--
AAAAGGHH!
AH, MUCH BETTER.
That was not very heroic of us.
OH, BUT I DISAGREE!
THOSE GUYS ARE EVIL, MAN-- THEY PREY ON PEOPLE'S WEAKNESSES! HOW MANY PEOPLE'S LIVES HAVE THEY RUINED? AND FOR WHAT?
MONEY. THAT'S WHAT.
AND ARE YOU JUST GONNA STAND THERE LOOKIN' SCARY? OR ARE YOU ACTUALLY GONNA SAY SOMETHING?

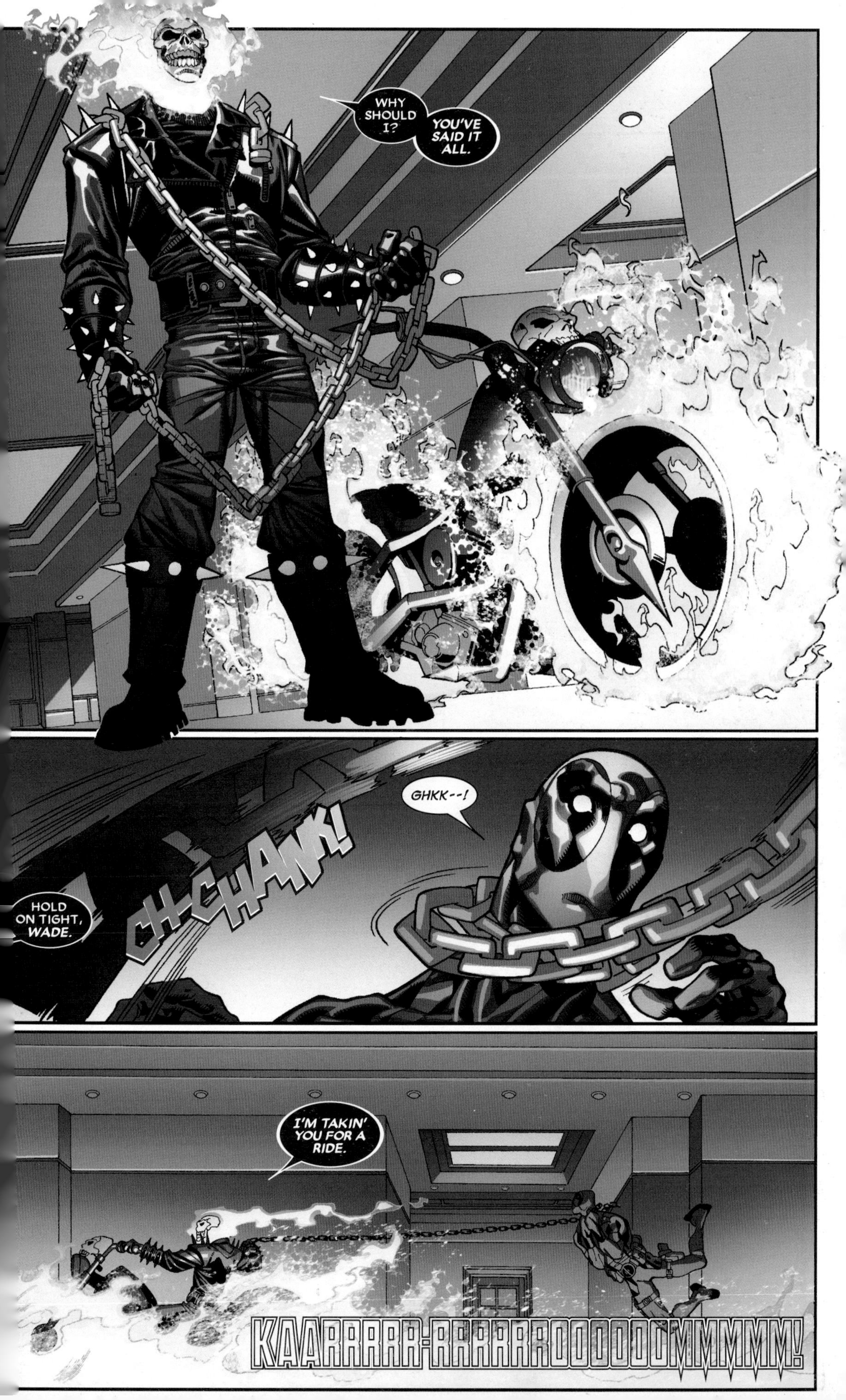
WHY SHOULD I?
YOU'VE SAID IT ALL.
GHKK--!
CH-CHANK!
HOLD ON TIGHT, WADE.
I'M TAKIN' YOU FOR A RIDE.
KAARRRRR-RRRRRROOOOOOMMMMMM!

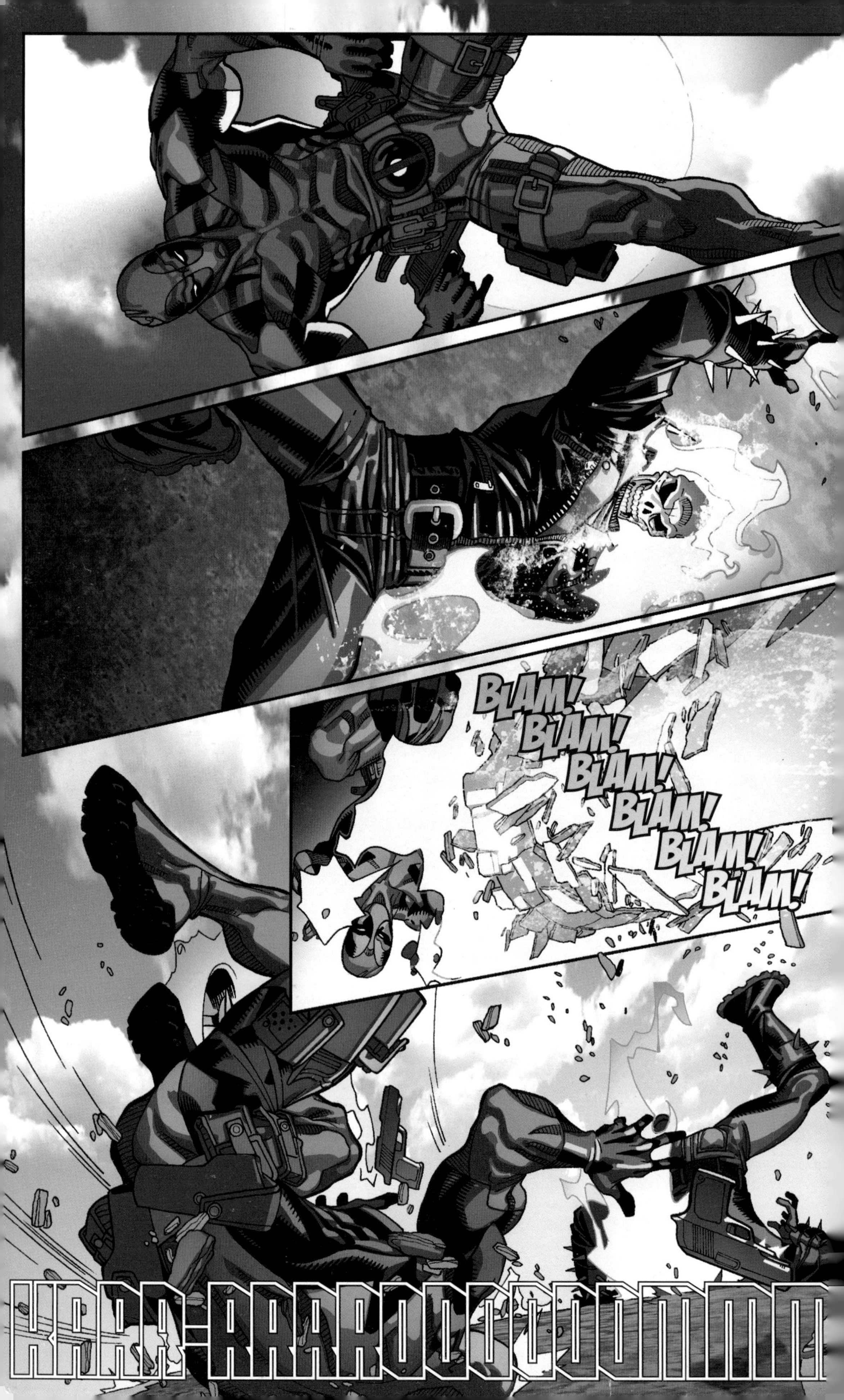
BLAM!
BLAM!
BLAM!
BLAM!
BLAM!
BLAM!
KRAA-AAAROOOCOOMMMM

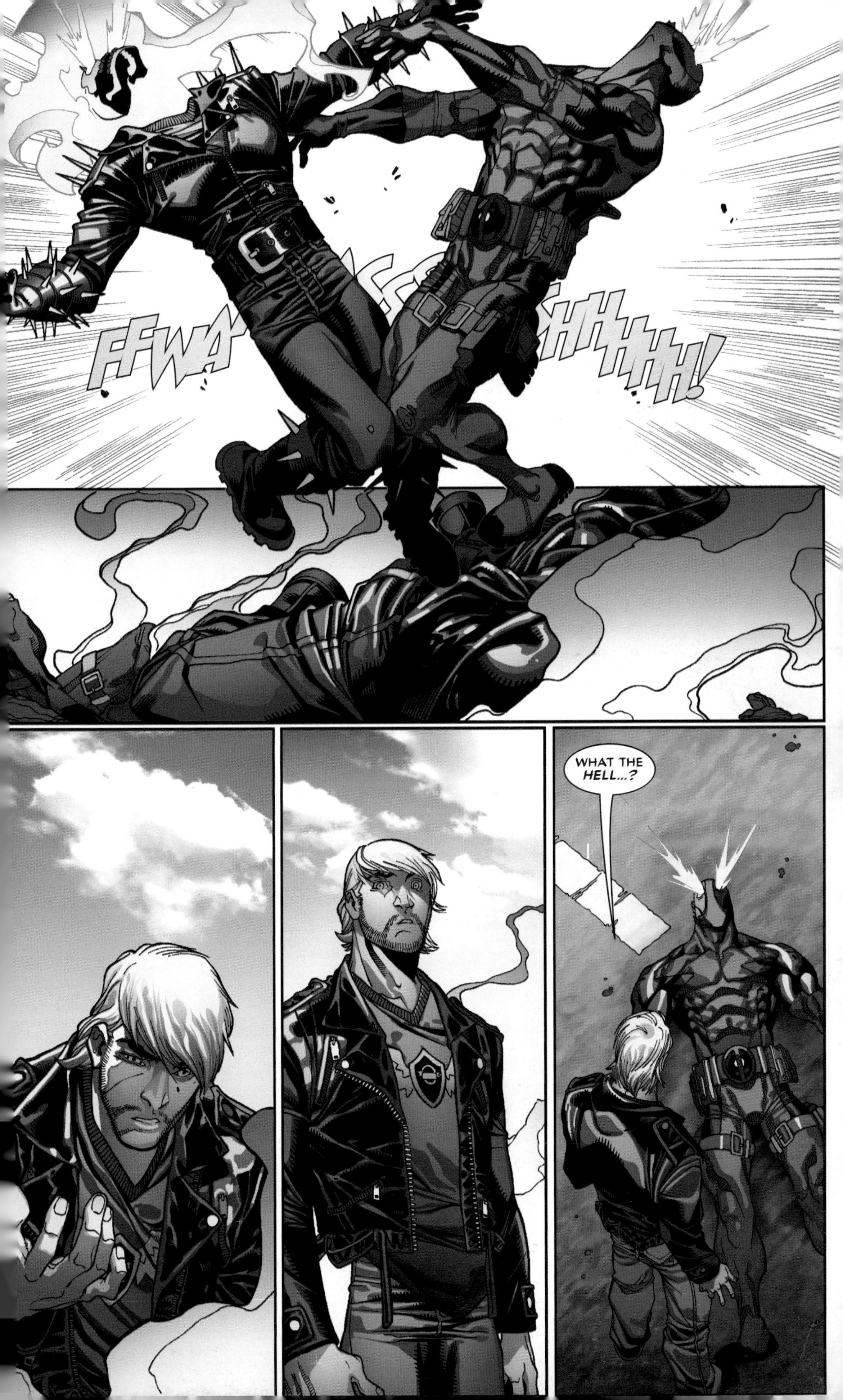
FFWASSHHHHHH!
WHAT THE HELL...?

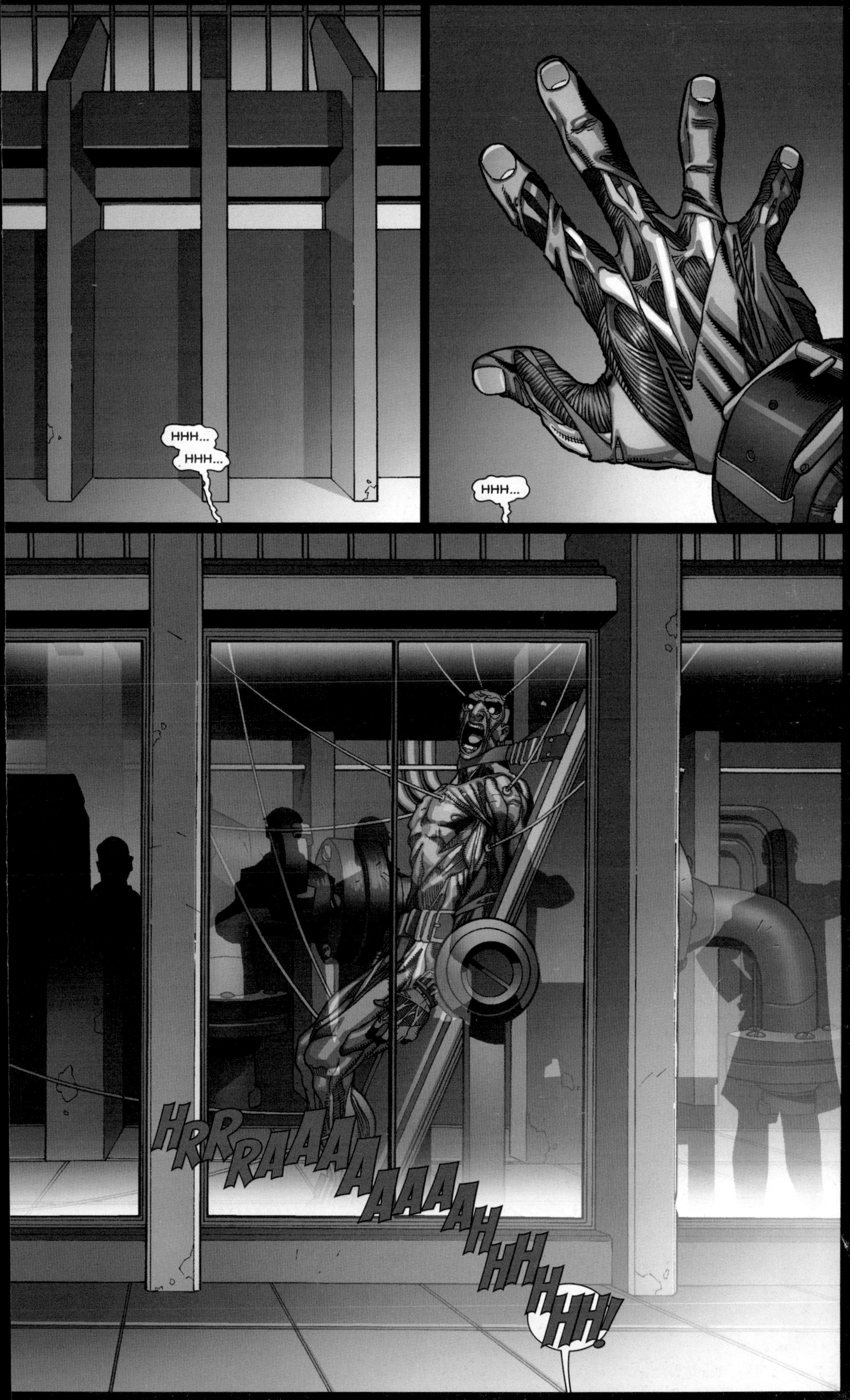
HHH...
HHH...
HHH...
HRRRAAAAAAAAAHHHHHHH!

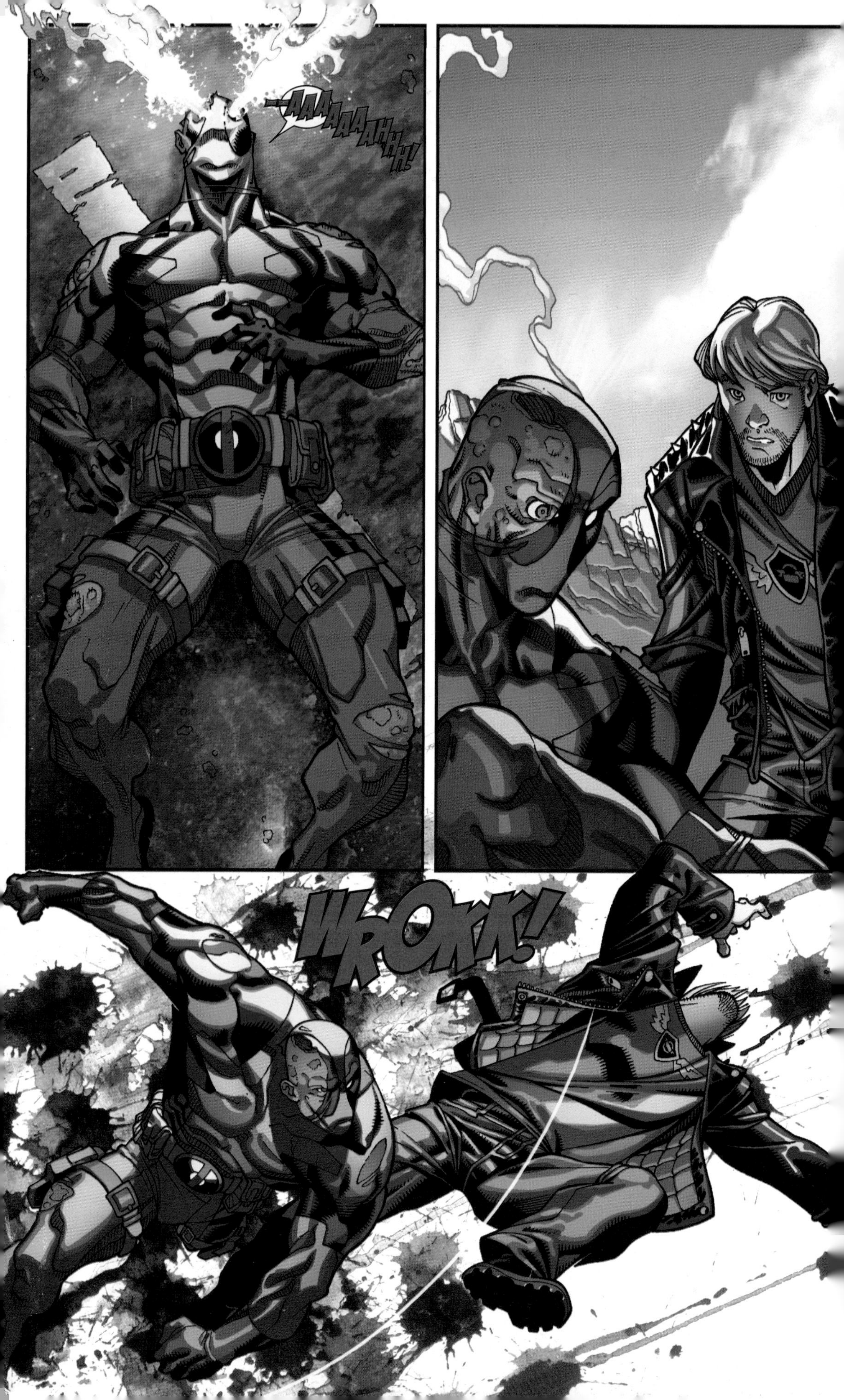

—AAAAAAAHHH!
WROKK!

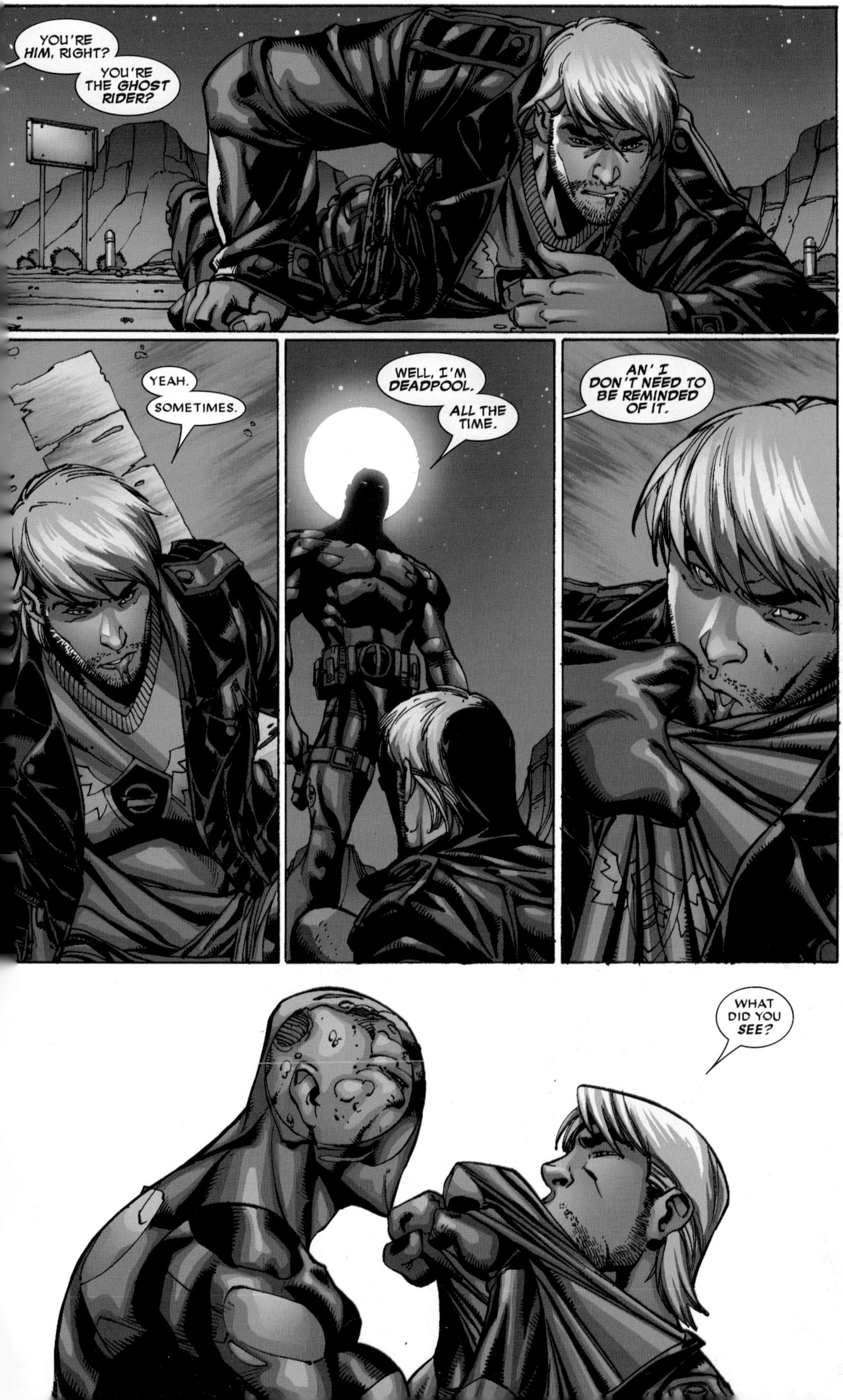
YOU'RE HIM, RIGHT?
YOU'RE THE GHOST RIDER?
YEAH.
SOMETIMES.
WELL, I'M DEADPOOL.
ALL THE TIME.
AN' I DON'T NEED TO BE REMINDED OF IT.
WHAT DID YOU SEE?

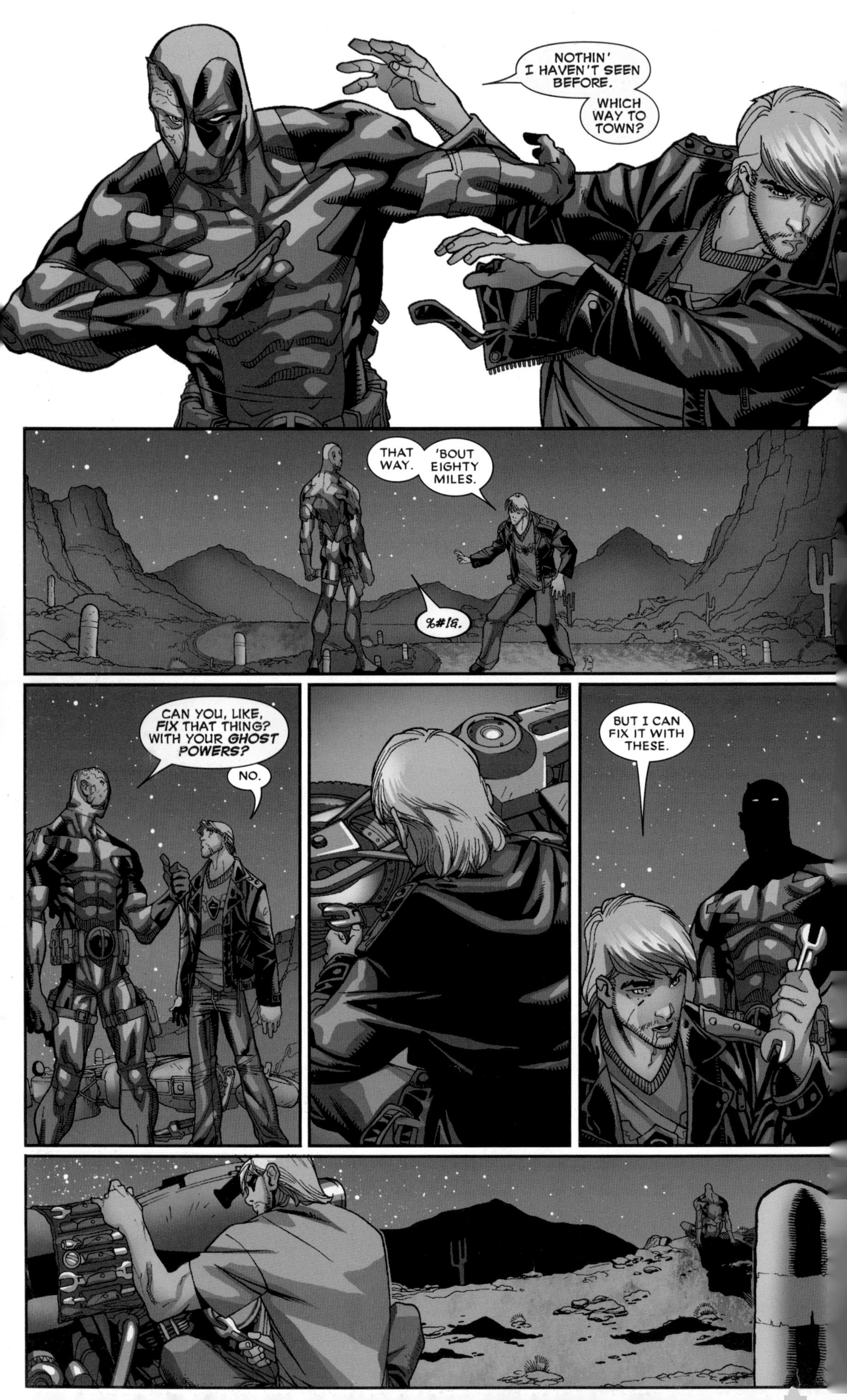
NOTHIN' I HAVEN'T SEEN BEFORE.
WHICH WAY TO TOWN?
THAT WAY.
'BOUT EIGHTY MILES.
%#!&.
CAN YOU, LIKE, FIX THAT THING? WITH YOUR GHOST POWERS?
NO.
BUT I CAN FIX IT WITH THESE.

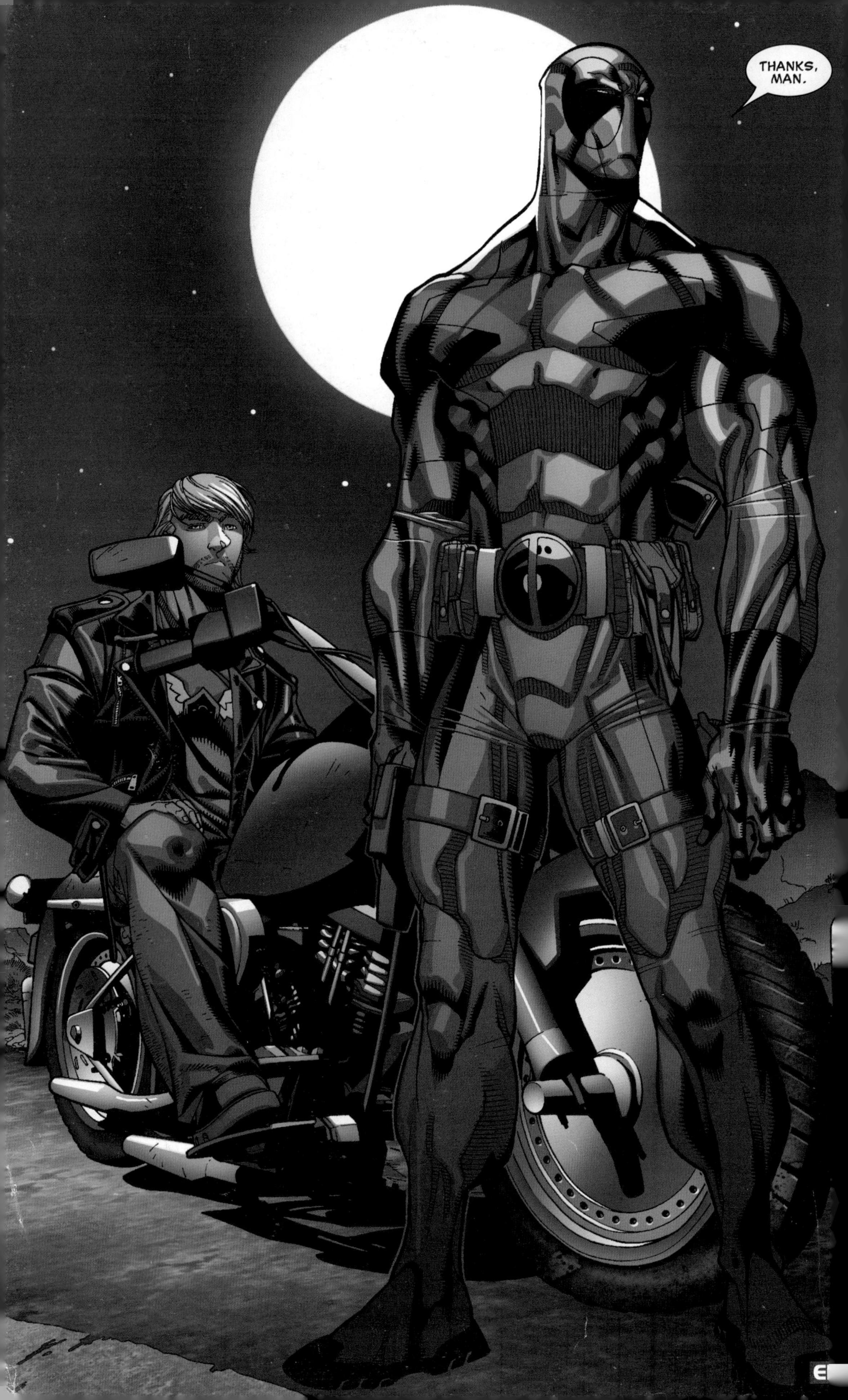
THANKS, MAN.

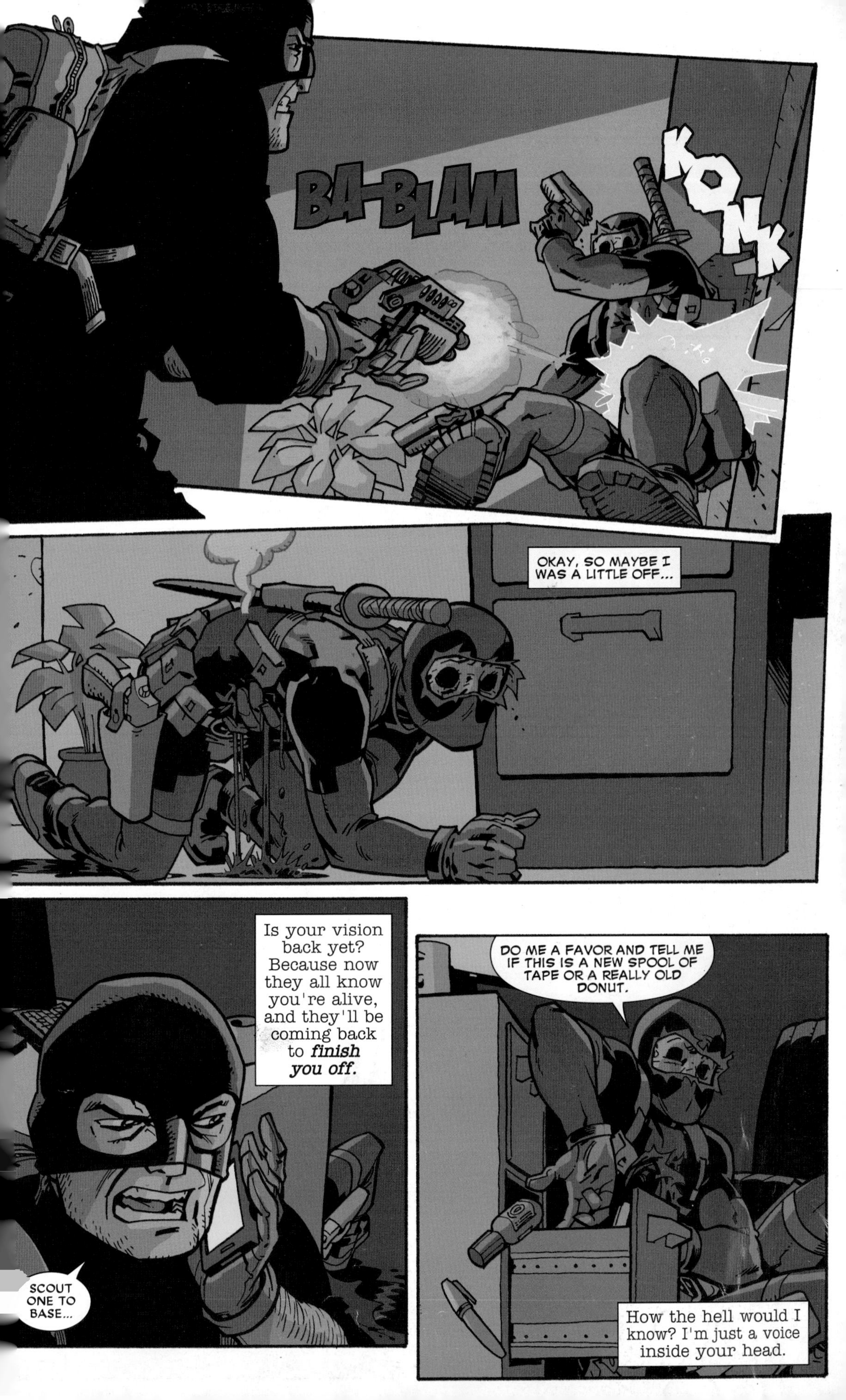
BA-BLAM
KONK
OKAY, SO MAYBE I WAS A LITTLE OFF...
Is your vision back yet? Because now they all know you're alive, and they'll be coming back to *finish you off.*
SCOUT ONE TO BASE...
DO ME A FAVOR AND TELL ME IF THIS IS A NEW SPOOL OF TAPE OR A REALLY OLD DONUT.
How the hell would I know? I'm just a voice inside your head.

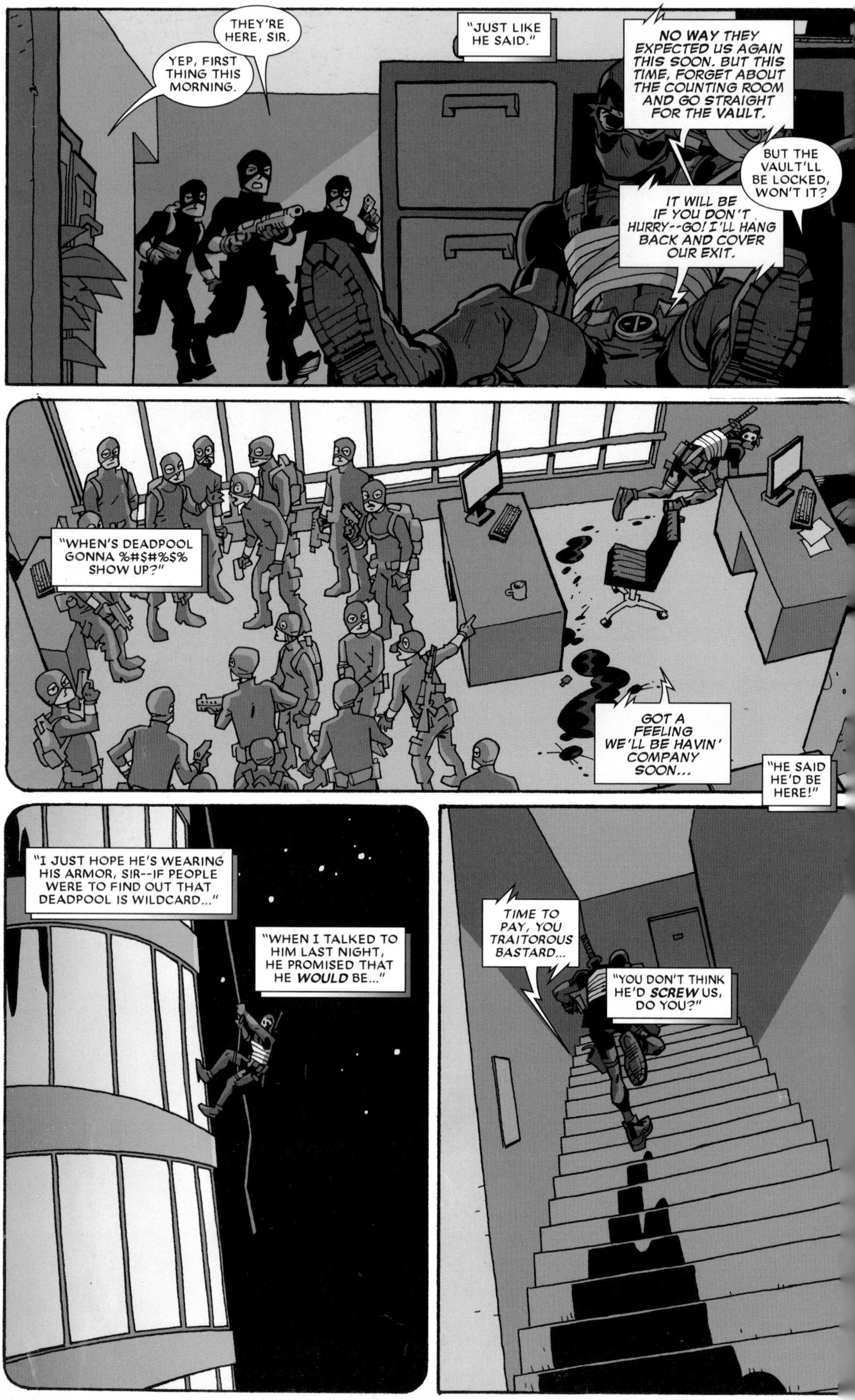
THEY'RE HERE, SIR.
YEP, FIRST THING THIS MORNING.
"JUST LIKE HE SAID."
NO WAY THEY EXPECTED US AGAIN THIS SOON. BUT THIS TIME, FORGET ABOUT THE COUNTING ROOM AND GO STRAIGHT FOR THE VAULT.
BUT THE VAULT'LL BE LOCKED, WON'T IT?
IT WILL BE IF YOU DON'T HURRY--GO! I'LL HANG BACK AND COVER OUR EXIT.
"WHEN'S DEADPOOL GONNA %#$#%$% SHOW UP?"
GOT A FEELING WE'LL BE HAVIN' COMPANY SOON...
"HE SAID HE'D BE HERE!"
"I JUST HOPE HE'S WEARING HIS ARMOR, SIR--IF PEOPLE WERE TO FIND OUT THAT DEADPOOL IS WILDCARD..."
"WHEN I TALKED TO HIM LAST NIGHT, HE PROMISED THAT HE WOULD BE..."
TIME TO PAY, YOU TRAITOROUS BASTARD...
"YOU DON'T THINK HE'D SCREW US, DO YOU?"

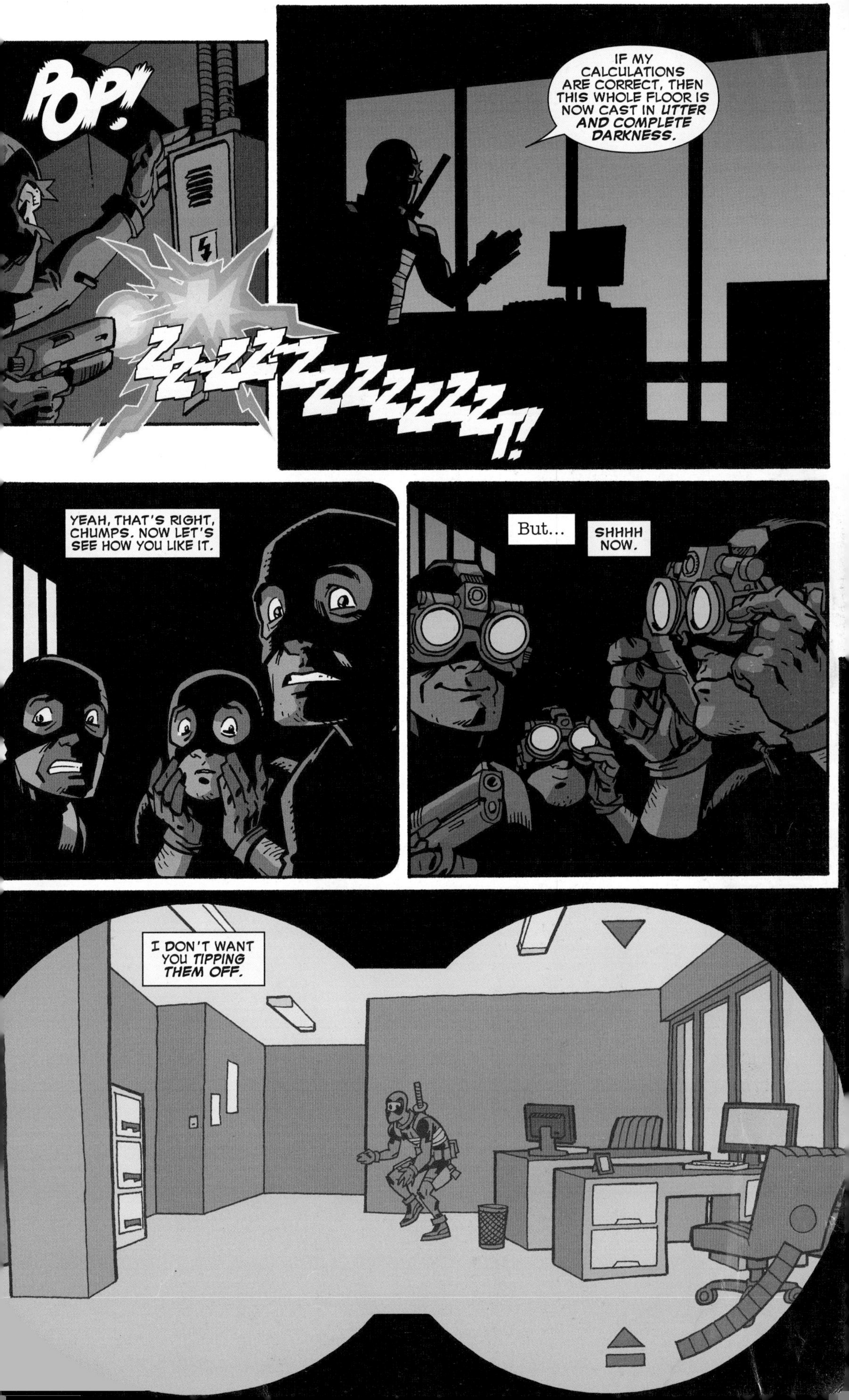
POP!
IF MY CALCULATIONS ARE CORRECT, THEN THIS WHOLE FLOOR IS NOW CAST IN UTTER AND COMPLETE DARKNESS.
ZZ-ZZZ-ZZZZZZZZZT!
YEAH, THAT'S RIGHT, CHUMPS. NOW LET'S SEE HOW YOU LIKE IT.
But...
SHHHH NOW.
I DON'T WANT YOU TIPPING THEM OFF.

WESTSIDE

STARBOARD

FOLD HERE

SECTION 4, ARTICLE 8

SLOT A

FOLD THERE

HEY KIDS! YOUR FAVORITE MERC WITH A MOUTH HERE TO GIVE YOU INSTRUCTIONS ON HOW TO ASSEMBLE YOUR **FREE*** 3-D GLASSES!!!

MATERIALS NEEDED:

1) A blade (non-rusty), sword, scissors or comparable cutting utensil

2) Glue (if you have glue, skip to step 5)

3) An old or lame horse

4) A big blender

5) A steady hand (non-severed)

INSTRUCTIONS:

A) Cut the pieces out around the edges

B) Fold the flaps on the earpieces, match them accordingly & glue

C) Allow glue to dry or let your little brother wear glasses then laugh as they dry to his face and he has to get them surgically removed!

D) Put on glasses and see the wonders of our 3-D cover come to life as you experience it in...
High Definition 4-D!

*After purchase of book! (We're not running a charity here, folks!)

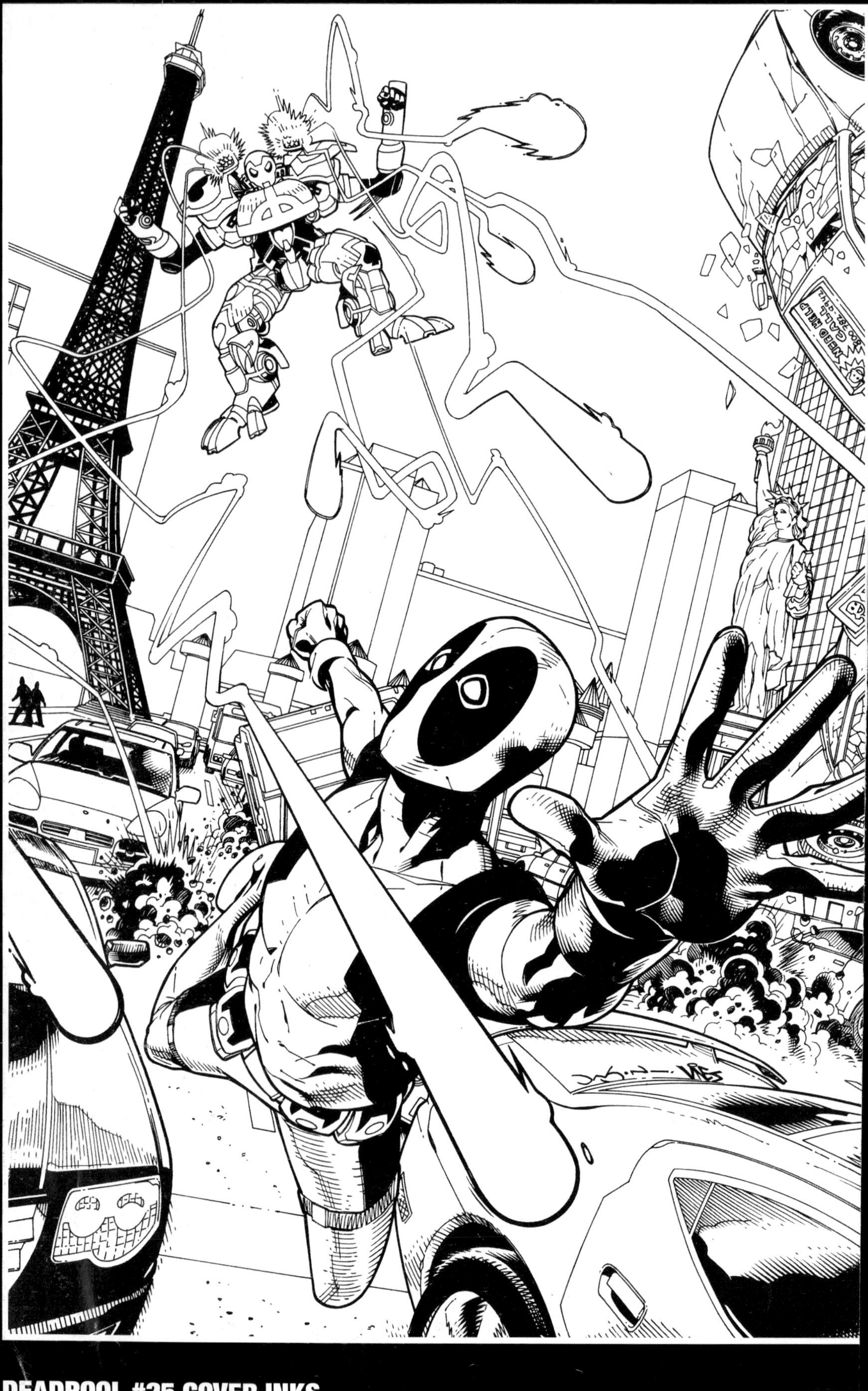

DEADPOOL #25 COVER INKS
by Dexter Vines

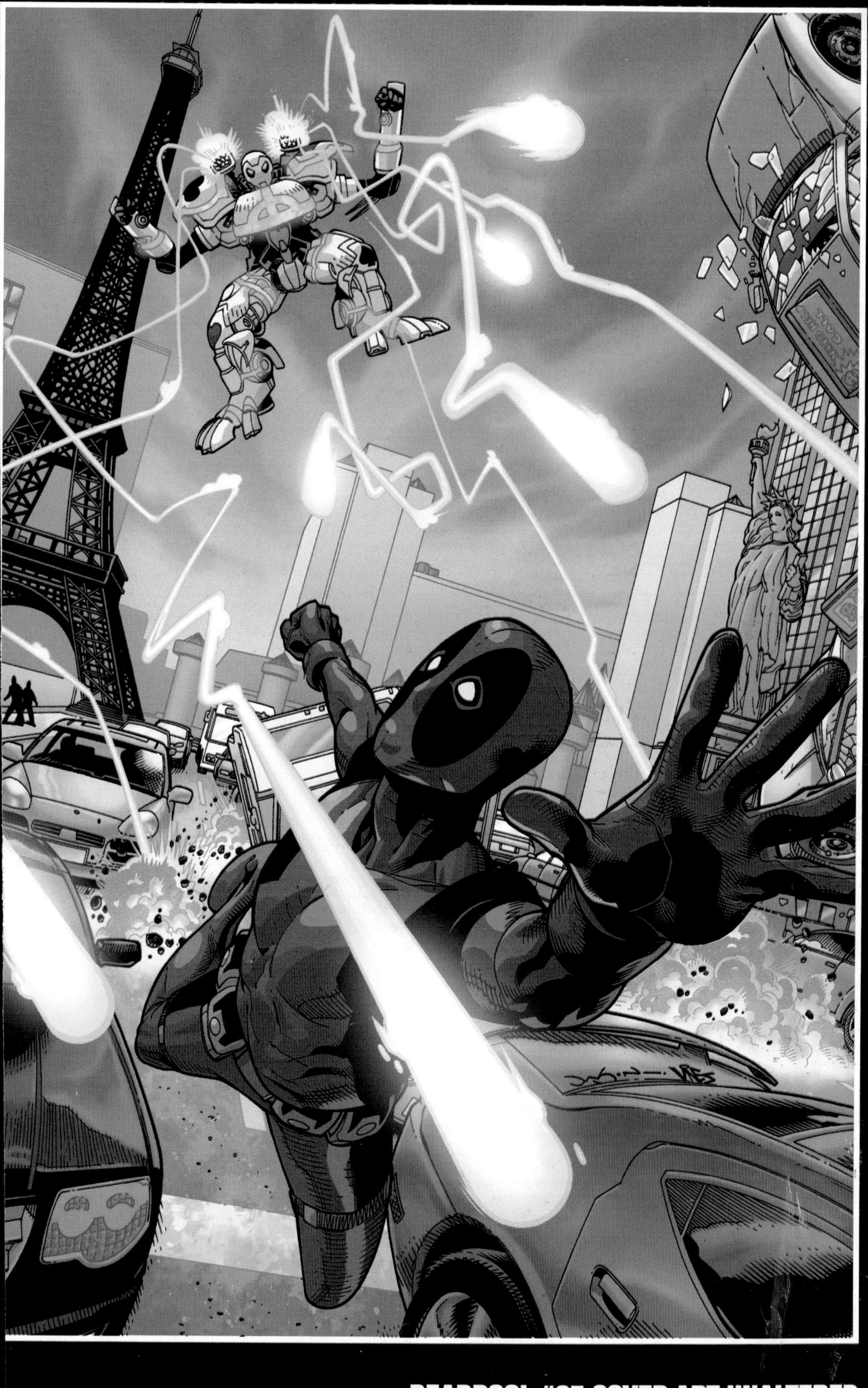

DEADPOOL #25 COVER ART UNALTERED
Colors by Dave Stewart

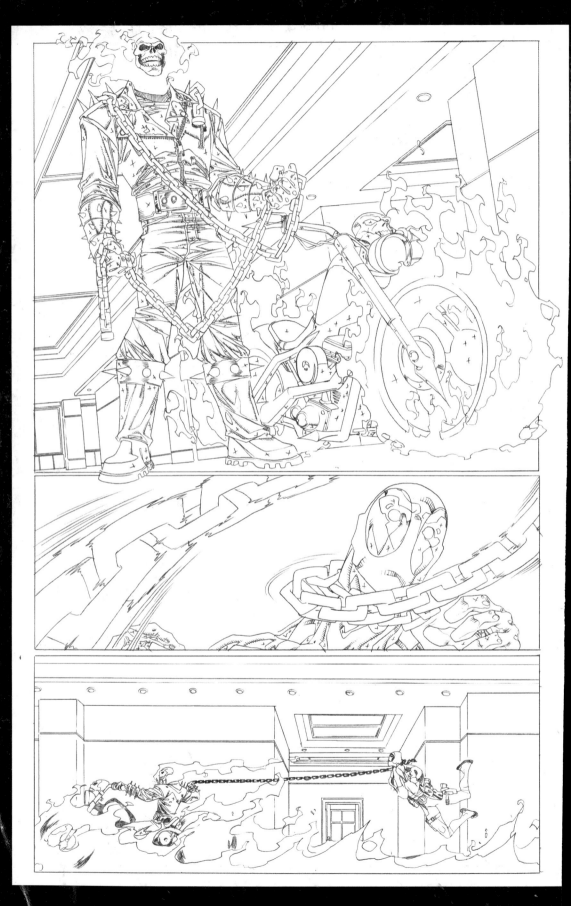

DEADPOOL #26, PAGE 5 PENCILS
by Carlo Barberi

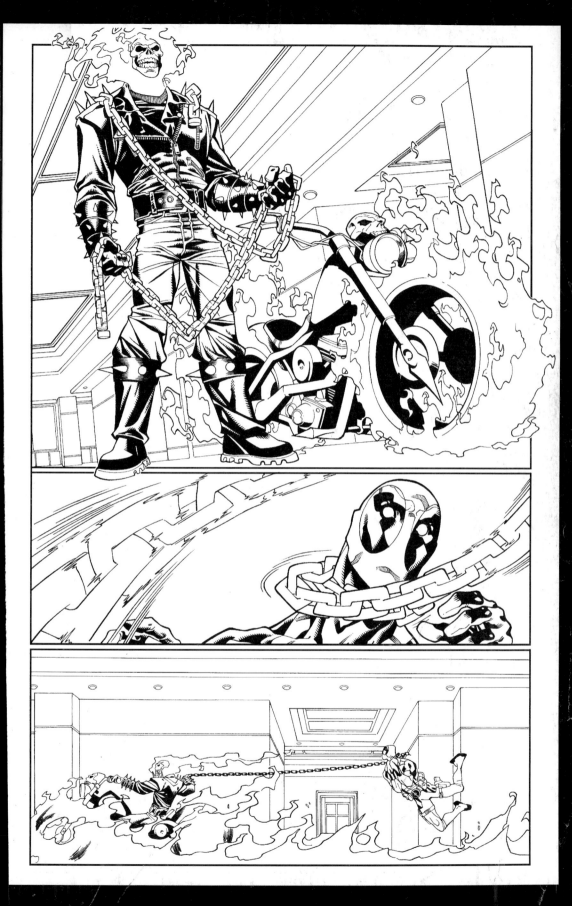

DEADPOOL #26, PAGE 5 INKS
by Juan Vlasco

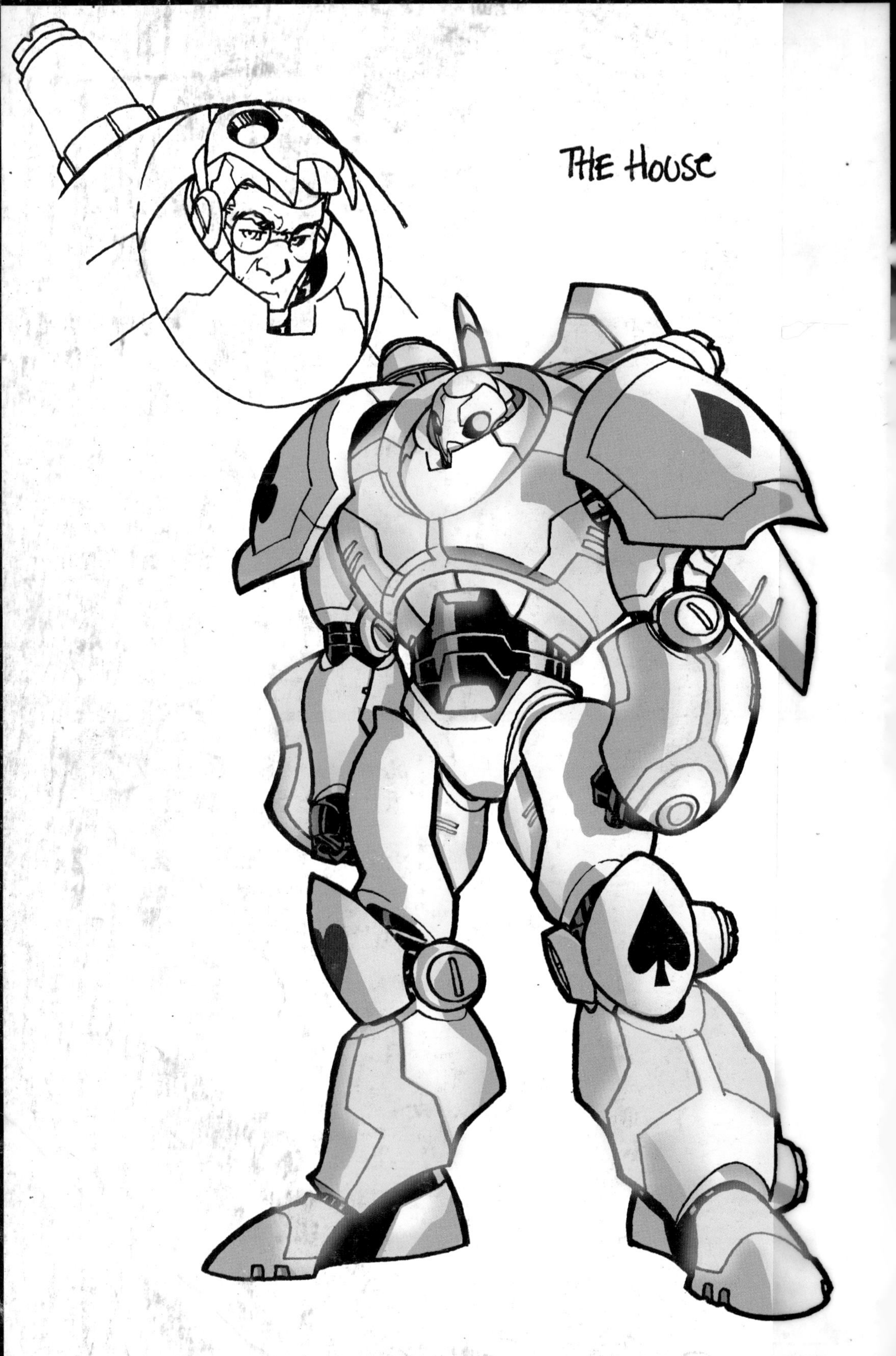
THE HOUSE

THE HOUSE CHARACTER DESIGN
by Carlo Barberi